AMERICAN QUESTION

IN ITS

NATIONAL ASPECT.

BEING ALSO

AN INCIDENTAL REPLY TO MR. H. R. HELPER'S "COMPENDIUM OF THE IMPENDING CRISIS OF THE SOUTH."

BY

ELIAS PEISSNER,

PROFESSOR IN UNION COLLEGE.

NEW YORK:
H. H. LLOYD & CO., PUBLISHERS,
25 HOWARD STREET.
1861.

Entered, according to Act of Congress, in the year 1861, by
ELIAS PEISSNER,
In the Clerk's Office of the District Court of the United States for the Southern District of New York.

DAVIES & KENT,
STEREOTYPERS AND ELECTROTYPERS,
113 *Nassau Street, N. Y.*

PREFACE.

SLAVERY, irrespective of its being right or wrong, is a historical fact, and depends as such, in its rise, growth, and decay, on the various circumstances of time and place which surround it, and have surrounded it, in different nations and periods. The soil, the climate, the geological and geographical congeniality with the most thickly settled countries of Europe, the large immigration consequent thereupon, the character of the settlers,—in short, land and people, production and population, made emancipation easier in our Northern States than in most of the Southern.

Therefore, we must censure those who wantonly throw all blame and all curses on the slaveholder as such; but we must also condemn the Slave-Politician who, on the natural circumstances unfavorable to speedy emancipation in the South, raised a play-ground for his political ambition and cast new obstacles in the way of freedom.

The imprudent abolitionist and the selfish politician exert a like influence upon the nation, though it be of different intensity. They rouse enmity and hatred between two sections of the same country; they, intentionally or unawares, render the Union less desirable and less honorable; they create fears, and threats, and experiments of dissolution.

For this their influence on Union and Nationality have we undertaken to review the course of the deadly antagonists. WITHIN the Union, then, alone the question of Slavery can be solved in such a manner as to bring permanently the greatest benefit to all parties concerned. This is, indeed, *the* American question, and it will haunt us whether there be a temporary dissolution of the Union or not. Slavery, far from being a sufficient reason for breaking the Union, adds new cause, new interest, new ties to draw us still more closely together.

To prove this is the object of the present treatise. Consequently, we have ventured to present in their proper light the two most famous arguments of the present day—the one taken from Political Economy, the other weeded out from history—and have endeavored to prove that they nowhere teach unrelenting hatred and disunion. Mr. H. R. HELPER's collection of figures and testimonies having become more popular than any other, we have taken his production as a basis for our First Two Books. The seriousness of the subject seemed at first to exclude all humor; but Mr. HELPER's passion and folly would, in some instances, have made any other treatment unfair and altogether unpalatable to the general reader.

In our Third Book we give Slavery its logical place in the progressive history of the world, and trace its *social* development within our own country, while in the Fourth Book we show its relation to the Union as a *political* body.

UNION COLLEGE, *Jan.* 8*th*, 1861.

CONTENTS.

BOOK I.

THE NUMBERS.

(IN REPLY TO CHAPTERS I., IX., X., XI., AND XII. OF MR. HELPER'S COMPENDIUM.)

I. The Science of Statistics.—II. False Impressions from True Numbers.—III. False Reasoning from True Numbers.—IV. New York and Norfolk.—V. New York and New Orleans.—VI. Louisiana and Massachusetts, New Orleans and Boston, Alabama and Maine.—VII. New York buys Virginia.—VIII. Imports and Exports combined of all the Principal Ports.—IX. Helper mistaking Years.—X. Helper ignoring Paupers and Criminals.—XI. Helper on Hay.—XII. Exhaustion of Lands and Hands.—XIII. The First Cause and Last Effect omitted by Helper in all his Arithmetical Reasonings.—XIV. Population, the Fundamental Cause of Production.—XV. Ratio of Increase of Population in Different Countries.—XVI. Ratio of the Natural and the Artificial Increase of the Population of the United States.—XVII. Ratio of Immigration in the Different States of the Union.—XVIII. Cause of the Difference.—XIX. Effect of Immigration on the Show-Tables of the South and the North.—XX. The Ultimate Effect of Production on Population.—XXI. The Negro Multiplying—his Show-Tables all Right.—XXII. Everybody Living Longer there where the "Niggers" are.—XXIII. The Posterior Part of Helper's Statistical Body.—XXIV. Conclusion......page 9

BOOK II.

THE TESTIMONIES.

(IN REPLY TO CHAPTERS III., IV., V., VI., VII., AND VIII. OF MR. HELPER'S COMPENDIUM.)

I. Single Testimonies.—II. The Chapters III. to IX. of Mr. Helper's Compendium.—III. The Testimony of the Union.—IV. The Testimony of England.—V. The Testimony of France.—VI. The Testimony of Germany.—VII. The Testimony of Russia.—VIII. The Testimony of Greece and Rome.—IX. The Testimony of the Churches and of the Bible.—X. The Testimony of Living Witnesses. — XI. General Remarks on the Testimonies.—XII. Mr. Helper's Bloody Plan.................................... 59

BOOK III.

THE DEVELOPMENT.

I. Slavery in History.—II. Negro Slavery in History.—III. Continuance of Negro Slavery in the Southern States.—IV. The Plea of the Curse.—V. The Plea of Race Inferiority.—VI. The Plea of Philanthropy.—VII. The Plea of Necessity.—VIII. The Plea of Self-Interest.—IX. The Plea of the Constitution.—X. Requisites for a Truly Philanthropic Emancipation : 1. Delicacy ; 2. Political Non-Interference with the South ; 3. Prudence.—XI. Actual Work already Accomplished in our Land : 1. Prohibition of the Slave-Trade ; 2. Abolition of Slavery ; 3. Spreading of the White Population ; 4. Amalgamation ; 5. Colonization.—XII. Conclusion........... 81

BOOK IV.

THE CRISIS.

I. Balance of Power.—II. Secession.—III. Our Policy.—IV. Integrity of the Union ; the National Property, Fortifications, Custom-Houses, etc. ; the Separate States : Texas ; California ; Louisiana ; the Border Slave States; Tennessee and Arkansas ; the two Carolinas, and the Western Gulf States.—V. Prognostic of a Southern Hexarchy.—VI. A Proposal for a new Compromise.—Conclusion........... 131

BOOK I.

THE NUMBERS.

THE AMERICAN QUESTION.

BOOK I.

THE NUMBERS.

IN REPLY TO CHAPTERS I., IX., X., XI., AND XII. OF MR. HELPER'S COMPENDIUM.

I.—THE SCIENCE OF STATISTICS.

We have taken as a basis of this first part of our treatise Mr. Helper's famous Numbers, by the aid of which he attempts to draw a new dividing line between two sections of the same country. These Numbers have become a sort of ground-work for popular reasoning on Union and Disunion. And *this* bearing alone is the cause of our attack. But before entering upon a special review of them, we will make a few general remarks.

The science of statistics is yet in its swaddling-clothes. Statistical accounts were kept in ancient times, but they referred principally to the government, and not to the nation at large. In the middle ages such accounts were entirely neglected; and what there were at any time had neither system nor order. In most modern times this science has grown, and especially during the present century; though even now the world and its philosophers are not agreed in respect to its limits or its definition.

A regular census of the population, to be repeated at fixed intervals, was first instituted by the United States, in the first year of its existence, and only since the beginning of this century have England and France followed our example. But what confusion reigns in these census tables, even in our modern times, may easily be seen from a few glances at their headings and diagrams, not to mention the single blunders which so frequently incur the censure of the common daily press.

F. B. HOUGH, the superintendent of the New York census in 1855, confesses in despair, " that it is, especially as it regards the *wealth* and *production* of the State, a labyrinth which we can not hope to be able to survey, unless a change is made in the whole system." What names shall we give to the censuses of other States, if that of New York is already seen to be " a labyrinth ?" But into such labyrinths Mr. HINTON ROWAN HELPER went groping for his numbers. No wonder he was lost, for Ariadne's thread seems not to have fallen to his lot.

H. F. BRACHELLI (one of those untiring German *savans* whose patient toiling remains ever a wonder to us Yankees as a class), in a recent statistical work on Germany, names several hundred volumes as his authorities, and adds, then, humbly : " I, of course, could only give *approximate* statements, and had to omit many things from want of sufficient data."

There is, indeed, no writer of any note, nor " any thorough scholar or profound thinker," who is not aware of the imperfect state of this science. Improvements are being made continually ; but, as yet, sufficient care is not taken in collecting the statistics, nor is there system in it, nor has any system been applied during periods sufficiently long to warrant all imaginable deductions and generalizations.

But all sciences, in their infancy, are somewhat presumptuous. And this is the case with the newly-invented science of statistics. Everything must now be reduced to numbers. Virtue, vice, morality, education, misery, happiness, slavery, freedom, love—all these vague and unmathematical quantities—must now be expressed in mathematical formulas. For there is no more quality: everything is quantity! This cant has, for a long time, been ringing in our ears, and Mr. HINTON ROWAN HELPER seems to be one of its modern trumpeters, though of the lower order.

Yet we must take men as they are, and, therefore, we will now view Mr. HELPER in his character as number-dealer.

II.—FALSE IMPRESSIONS FROM TRUE NUMBERS.

We must take men as they are, and we must also take numbers as they are. We will now suppose that the numbers which Mr. HELPER extracts from official reports, and those which we ourselves will draw from similar sources, are all true and correct. They are all—let us suppose—exact numerical expressions of real facts. Now let us give a few examples, to see what the impressions are which these true numbers may make on our minds. We take them from the Official Census of the United States, 1850.

TABLE I.—THE DEAF AND DUMB, BLIND, LAME, INSANE, AND IDIOTIC PERSONS IN NEW YORK AND VIRGINIA.

State of New York	6,630
State of Virginia	3,675

This is a very nice statistical table, and quite characteristic of the science of statistics. "The deaf and dumb, blind, insane, and idiotic persons," like the Living Witnesses, are all huddled together in one company. A happy family, indeed!

After we had recovered somewhat from the shock the presence of such a variety of cripples naturally caused, we looked again at the figures, all told and positive. At first sight—and this is the only sight men often take—New York seems to have almost twice as many "deaf and dumb, blind, insane, and idiotic persons" as Virginia. And we did, indeed, set ourselves at work to bewail the glorious Empire State, which, in spite of its freedom, was getting so distressingly blind and insane, and deaf, and idiotic, and dumb, while darkened Virginia saw and heard, and thought and spoke in a ratio so much greater.

Now, there is nothing so very unfair in this example. We get about the same impression from many of Mr. Helper's tables, and his bewailings are often not based on firmer ground. But let us look at one of *his* examples:

TABLE II.—THE EXPORTS OF NEW YORK AND VIRGINIA.

Mr. Helper states that the exports in 1852 amounted (in round numbers for popular use),

```
In New York to........................$87,484,000
In Virginia to..........................  2,505,000
```

A common man compares these two numbers and exclaims: "Alas! Virginia has forty times less exports than New York!" Now let us but add the comparative population of the two States:

```
New York, 1850..........................3,097,000
Virginia, 1850..........................1,421,000
```

And, without going into any further reasoning, but by

only finding the proportions of the exports to the number of inhabitants, our wonder and surprise would be reduced at least fifty per cent. We will soon give more examples; but we have first another observation to make, intimately connected with all these numerical parades.

III.—FALSE REASONING FROM TRUE NUMBERS.

No one doubts that there must be a cause for these special facts and their representative numbers, and indeed a cause for just what they are. We mean, they must be the result of some agent, or the consequence of some prior principle; and we must see, too, that the numbers may all be correct, singly and added, but still we may mistake their cause or causes, mistake the relations of several such numerical tables, mistake their consequences, and at last their effect on man. For man is, after all, the end of the whole song of numbers and notes. There seem, then, to be some difficulties in the way of using and explaining numbers; but Mr. HELPER does not think so. He has an improved *camera obscura*, a kind of a dark-lantern or "nigger" glass, which, showing everything in the same swarthy hue, gives at once the cause for everything, seen or unseen; and that is, by-the-by, the only glass he ever uses. While thus we others, poor mortals, must break our heads, and think, and compare, and study, and observe, he simply looks through his mysterious glass and exclaims: "Slavery!" and all difficulties vanish at once. We envy the man for his time-and-labor-saving machine, but can not refrain from giving our curious readers a few examples, to show in what a peculiar way it works. We are tempted to believe that its balance-wheel is a little out of order.

IV.—NEW YORK AND NORFOLK.

The wise Governor of Virginia extols, as Mr. HELPER quotes, the bygone trophies of the harbor of Norfolk, and laments its present miserable condition, numbers ever being added to demonstrate and to prove. Now, there is many a harbor on the long coast of the Atlantic which has met with a similar fortune, both South and North. It was prophesied that New York would become "the center of trade and great emporium of North America," and even of the whole Western world, long, long ago—long before Governor WISE bewailed his country—at a period, indeed, when the enslaved children of innocent darkness were still gracing the shores and streets of New Amsterdam. The James River is no Hudson, and the Alleghanies are no Palisades. The lakes of the North, too, have some little influence on commerce. We might as well compare London with Norwich. But still Mr. HELPER uses his dark machine, looks through the glass, and answers: "Slavery!" Now, does Mr. HINTON ROWAN HELPER really think that, if Virginia had emancipated her slaves as soon as New York, the proportion between the commerce of Norfolk and that of New York would have still been the same in 1850 as it was in 1790? Or, that "the direct foreign trade of Norfolk would still exceed that of the city of New York?" Or, that Virginia would still "stand preeminently the first commercial State of the Union?" Or, "that her commerce would still exceed in amount that of all the New England States combined?" No, we can not think him lacking thus much in judgment. But still, his statistical exhibitions would lead to such conclusions, and he himself must have had similar impressions when he turned away from the picture he had drawn of the two States, "with feelings mingled with indignation and disgust."

V.—NEW YORK AND NEW ORLEANS.

But why did Mr. HELPER not take the statistics of New Orleans and compare them with those of New York? This would have been, in every respect, a fairer comparison than New York and Norfolk. New Orleans is the great outlet of the Mississippi, the principal point of attraction for the South and West; New York a similar magnet for the North, East, and Northwest. Now let us see the exports of the one and of the other, not forgetting, however, that New York now rules, and will probably rule for many years to come, over the largest productive area of the United States.

TABLE III.—EXPORTS AND IMPORTS.

[*From the "Annuaire de l'Economie Politique et de la Statistique," Paris*, 1859.]
[The table refers to the year 1857—at least we think so, from comparing some of its general items with the report of the Secretary of the Treasury of the United States for that year.]

Total exports of the United States	$338,985,000
Total exports of New York	111,029,000
Total exports of New Orleans	91,536,000
Total exports of Boston and Charlestown	24,894,000
Total exports of Mobile	20,575,000

This is the order of the cities in amount of goods exported. In this table New Orleans is the second, and, indeed, comes very near to New York. Would not this give a fairer and more respectable picture than New York and Norfolk? Or, let us take the imports, according to the same document:

Total imports of the United States	$360,890,000
Total imports of New York	222,550,000
Total imports of 31 States (exc. New York)	148,340,000
Total imports of Boston and Charlestown	44,840,000
Total imports of New Orleans	24,891,000
Total imports of Philadelphia	17,850,000

We see from this table that New York takes two thirds of all the imports of the United States, and New Orleans comes immediately after Boston, and before Philadelphia. At any rate, this would again have been a fairer comparison than New York and Virginia, South Carolina and Pennsylvania, North Carolina and Massachusetts.

But let us imitate Mr. HELPER.

VI.—LOUISIANA AND MASSACHUSETTS—NEW ORLEANS AND BOSTON—ALABAMA AND MAINE.

TABLE IV.—VALUE OF EXPORTS FROM 1856 TO 1857.

[*From the official report of the Treasurer of the United States.*]

Exports of Louisiana (Slave State)	$91,894,000
Exports of Massachusetts (Free State)	30,146,000
Exports of New Orleans (Slave)	91,536,000
Exports of Boston and Charlestown (Free)	24,894,000
Exports of Alabama (Slave)	20,576,000
Exports of Maine (Free)	3,716,000

There is that negro-loving Massachusetts, of good old Puritan stock, with its manufacturing palaces and its spacious port! There is Northern Maine, with its immeasurable natural wealth and its magnificent harbor! And still the poor Slave States are ahead of them! Neither the elevation of modern Athens nor the depth of Portland can stifle "our indignation and disgust!" But the picture would become still more alarming if we added some items of population. We have not the populations of 1857 at hand, and therefore we must be content to give those of 1850. The numbers would now be different, but the ratios would not vary much.

Population of the State of Louisiana	517,000
Population of the State of Massachusetts	994,000

Louisiana had already three times as many dollars of exports as Massachusetts; but the comparison of their populations would double the ratio.

Oh, thou unfortunate Massachusetts! twice three times below thy Slave sister on the Mississippi! Thou sunkest so low probably because, in days of yore, thou burnedst with Puritan zeal those four innocent Quakers, in rashness the prototypes of thy Abolitionists!

And thou, thrice unhappy Boston, Charlestown included, free white and free colored, and still $70,000,000 behind the Slave city of New Orleans! Why didst thou emancipate Mum Bet? That first free "nigger" girl of the North is the cause of all thy shortcoming!

But this would be Helper's logic and Hinton Rowan's rhetoric, and we abstain from indulging longer in those articles.

Let us open his own show-tables again!

VII.—NEW YORK BUYS VIRGINIA.

Mr. Helper had probably his numerical hosts continually before his eyes, and sometimes accidentally combined one item with another, and then made a comparison without "jumping exactly at conclusions." Thus he saw the numbers which express the real and personal wealth of the city of New York, and somewhere in their vicinity the numbers of Virginia. "Well," says he, "what do you think of that? The city of New York could buy the whole State of Virginia!" Now, what is Mr. Helper's purpose? Why his surprise? Is that all due to Slavery? Are there no other rich cities in the world? The wealth of a whole nation often concentrates in a city. There is no Negro Slavery in England; but they say London could easily buy one or two provinces of its own—New York and a few European kingdoms included.

VIII.—IMPORTS AND EXPORTS COMBINED OF ALL THE PRINCIPAL PORTS.

Fighting, with numbers as arms, seems, after all, a pleasant exercise. It fastens the interest, and while it amuses, it strengthens the Constitution. We must continue this prelude a little longer.

TABLE V.—TOTAL IMPORTS AND EXPORTS.

[*From the "Annuaire" (quoted above*).]

Of the United States	$723,850,000
New York	346,939,000
New Orleans	116,784,000
Boston and Charlestown	73,167,000
Charleston, S. C.	30,023,000
Philadelphia	24,985,000
Baltimore	24,287,000
San Francisco	23,566,000
Mobile	21,485,000
Oswego, Champlain, and Lakes	18,123,000
Savannah	11,450,000
Richmond	6,600,000

There, Mr. HELPER, are the principal ports of all our States, Free and Slave. They stand there, all in order, according to their merits—old grandmother New York at the head. But do you not see that her children follow her peaceably, one after the other—first a black one and then a white one? Do you not see, too, that New Orleans has indeed grown to be rather a big boy, though raised down South, where the "niggers" are? Why will you come and disturb this order and harmony between children of the same mother, who walk along dressed in numbers more harmonious than the planets even?

But Mr. HELPER has somewhat the nature of a comet, and hence his disturbing influence. Before we lose sight of him entirely, we may point out a few more of his eccentricities.

IX.—HELPER MISTAKING YEARS.*

Mr. HELPER, in his first comparisons, which were to prepare the way for all "indignation and disgust," chose not only three Free States which are generally considered as the most wealthy and populous of the whole Union, and compared them with three Slave States which show, according to the United States census, the least growth; but, in order to make the "disparities" still more "degrading," he selected just those years which best suited his "patriotic purpose." Thus, in his comparison of the imports and exports of New York and Virginia, he saw fit to give the exports of 1852 instead of 1853—Virginia's tables showing, in the former year, $1,000,000 less than in the latter, and New York $21,000,000 more. Immediately afterward, in the table of imports, he changed again to 1853, New York having imported in that year $46,000,000 more than in 1852, and Virginia $336,854 less. He draws quite liberally on the uneven treasures of 1852, 1853, 1854, and 1855. Sometimes, too, he mistakes States for Cities, and *vice versa*. Thus, he does not compare the exports of Pennsylvania and South Carolina, as he does of New York, Virginia, Massachusetts, and North Carolina; but he takes Charleston and Philadelphia. The States, however, would give the following results:

	Pennsylvania.	South Carolina.
Imports in 1791	$3,436,000	$2,693,000
Imports in 1853	6,255,000	15,400,000

The strongest Pro-Slavery State would compare too well in that respect.

---

* Several tables and estimates were thankfully received by the author from S. BARSTOW, a student in Union College. The numbers 9, 10, 11 are based upon a selection of them.

But why did the impartial "patriot" not compare Maine and Georgia, Michigan and Missouri, Connecticut and Kentucky, which would have given much fairer results? They would have been altogether fairer States to be compared with each other, in regard to extent, natural advantages, and history. The educational statistics, especially, would have confounded Mr. Helper's universal argument.

X.—HELPER IGNORING PAUPERS AND CRIMINALS.

But to his six States Mr. Helper might well have added some statistics about pauperism and criminality, things which are regarded by some to be as sure an index of the state of society as the amount of hay and hemp produced. We may supply here that little oversight.

TABLE VI.—WHOLE NUMBER OF PAUPERS SUPPORTED AND CRIMINALS CONVICTED WITHIN THE YEAR 1850.

PAUPERS.

States.	Population.	Paupers.	Proportion.
New York	3,097,000	39,835	1 in 50
Virginia	1,421,000	5,118	1 in 200
Massachusetts	904,000	15,777	1 in 60
North Carolina	869,000	1,931	1 in 400
Pennsylvania	2,311,000	11,550	1 in 200
South Carolina	668,000	1,642	1 in 400

CRIMINALS.

States.	Population.	Criminals.	Proportion.
New York	3,097,000	10,279	1 in 300
Virginia	1,421,000	107	1 in 13,000
Massachusetts	990,000	7,250	1 in 1,200
North Carolina	869,000	647	1 in 1,300
Pennsylvania	2,311,000	858	1 in 3,000
South Carolina	668,000	46	1 in 14,000

But we know well that the result of such comparisons would destroy the symmetry of the artistico-statistical work of the patriot, and on that ground he may be pardoned by an art-loving community.

XI.—HELPER ON HAY.

"We can now prove," Mr. H. says, "and we shall now proceed to prove, that the annual hay crop of the Free States is worth considerable more, in dollars and cents, than all the cotton, tobacco, rice, hay, hemp, and cane-sugar annually produced in the fifteen Slave States." He quite liberally gives $11 as the average value of a ton of hay, and produces the following recapitulation:

Hay crop of Free States..................$142,138,998
Sundry products of Slave States........... 138,605,723

Balance in favor of Free States........ $3,533,275

Now, the tables and estimates of Prof. De Bow, "the able and courteous Superintendent," are quite different. According to *his* Compendium of the Census of 1850, we find the average price of hay to be *seven* dollars, and that of the other products differing in a similar way from Helper's "impartial" estimates. (See tables CLXXXVI. and CXX. of the United States Census.) Our recapitulation would then present the following figures:

Hay crop of Free States.................. $88,836,874
Sundry products of Slave States 141,100,081

Balance in favor of the South $52,263,807

The value of the cotton crop of 1850 alone exceeded, according to Prof. De Bow's tables, the hay crop of the North by $2,000,000. In a similar way might other tables be modified. Bushel Measure Products would appear as follows:

Free States $276,839,041
Slave States............................ 244,770,070

Balance in favor of the North $32,069,041
Instead of Mr. Helper's.................. 44,782,636

And the Pound Measure Products would present the following table:

```
Free States ........................... $151,260,408
Slave States........................... 155,648,222
                                        _____
    Balance in favor of the South........  $4,387,814
    Instead of Helper's in favor of the North..  59,199,108
```

Besides, the agricultural home manufactures show, according to Prof. DE BOW, a balance in favor of the South by more than $8,000,000, which might be added to the bushels or pounds of the South. The District of Columbia, too, is mentioned there as of some little value, while in the eyes of the tabulating Mr. HELPER it is a perfect nonentity. But we must abstain from further particulars.

XII.—EXHAUSTION OF LANDS AND HANDS.

We have pointed out some of the modifications of which Mr. HELPER's numbers are susceptible, though we consider them one by one. These were, however, but a few skirmishes among the outposts, of little advantage to either side. We now begin to make more wholesale work of them, though the main battle is not yet on hand.

Mr. HELPER speaks of the exhaustion of the South; but his words and conclusions might just as well be applied to the whole Union. We all—Slave States and Free States, North and South—are exhausting our lands and our hands, our soil and our labor, our agriculture and our general industry. We take all the different branches of industry together, because they are as intimately and naturally connected as the members of our physical bodies. An injury done to one is an injury done to all. The time is gradually passing away in which party politicians can further arouse and excite the producer against the manufacturer, or the merchant against either. We begin to understand that their interests are the same. Long before BASTIAT published his *Harmonies Economiques*, this principle was anticipated. The systematic exposition of it by modern economists can leave no doubt in the mind of the impartial student as to its merits. Let us be glad that the dark times of industrial enmity are coming to an end! There is no truth in the old saying, "What one gains, another must lose!" Our earth is not a pandemonium. Only as long as men are ignorant of their true self-interest, is there a "*bellum omnium adversus omnes*"—a war of everybody against everybody. As society advances and civilization grows, the great principle of harmony is perceived to reign over all that concerns matter or man.

Let us now refer to our own H. C. CAREY, and see some of the applications of this principle to the United States. We can not do better than to use his own language, for he is the acknowledged apostle of this "harmony of interests." He has directed all the powers of his mind toward that one great principle, and has expounded it with an energy almost bordering on monomania. We have so much the more a right to quote him, as he, too, has written statistical works, and also a volume on Slavery. In his LETTER X. to President BUCHANAN, he says:

"Throughout the larger portion of the Union the market is distant hundreds and thousands of miles, and the consequences are seen in the fact that the soil is becoming almost everywhere exhausted—wealth thus diminishing when it should increase.

"How it diminishes has recently been shown by an eminent agriculturist, from whom we learn:

"That the potash and phosphoric acid annually taken from the land is worth, at the usual market-price of these commodities, nearly $20,000,000—scarcely any of which is ever returned.

"That the ashes of 600,000,000 bushels of corn are annually taken from the soil—scarcely any of which are ever returned.

"That the total annual waste of the mineral constituents of food is 'equal to 1,500,000,000 bushels of corn.'

"'To suppose,' says the author of these estimates—'to suppose that this state of things can continue, and we, as a nation, remain prosperous, is simply ridiculous. We have as yet much virgin soil, but it will not be long ere we reap the reward of our present improvidence. It is merely a question of time, and time will solve the problem in a most unmistakable manner. What with our earth-butchery and prodigality, we are each year losing the intrinsic essence of our vitality.

"'Our country has not yet grown feeble from this loss of its life-blood, but *the hour is fixed when, if our present system continue, the last throb of the nation's heart will have ceased, and when America, Greece, and Rome will stand together among the ruins of the past.*

"'The question of economy should be, not, How much do we annually produce, but, How much of our annual productions is saved to the soil? Labor employed in robbing the earth of its capital stock of fertilizing matter, is worse than labor thrown away. In the latter case, it is a loss to the present generation; in the former, it becomes an inheritance of poverty for our successors. Man is but a tenant of the soil, and he is guilty of a crime when he reduces its value for other tenants who are to come after him.'

"Waste, such as is here described, Mr. President, *is* a crime, and it finds its punishment in the natural, moral, and political decline, to which your attention has now been called. Look almost where the traveler may, he is struck with the wretched condition of that which, in this country, is called agriculture, but which, in the civilized countries of Europe, would be denominated pure and simple robbery of the great bank given by the Creator for the use of man. Its effects are shown in the facts that, in New York, where eighty years since twenty-five to thirty bushels of wheat were an ordinary crop, the average is now only fourteen, while that of Indian corn is but twenty-five. In Ohio, a State that but half a century since was a wilderness, the average of wheat is less than twelve; and it diminishes when it should increase. Throughout the West the process of exhaustion is everywhere going on; the large crops of the early period of a settlement being followed invariably by smaller ones in later years."

You may call this a dark picture, or a gloomy prophecy. But it is the same that LIEBIG but lately pointed to, from his far-famed laboratory. It is the same that FR. LIST has deduced from history. It is the same that PROUDHON reads in Socialism, when he says: "Of what account can all consolidations of property and artificial manurings be against such a radical exhaustion!" It is the result of that suicidal policy "which first exports food and then men"—that drives the son from his home and sends him to seek his fortune in distant lands—that scatters a population over extensive wastes of land and makes it descend in the scale of civilization—that disregards the value of productive power, and looks only at momentary production and gain —a policy which is ever doomed to pant and to reach after more lands, though the old homesteads might harbor a hundred millions more. It is, indeed, excusable if our countrymen, ashamed of their nation's decay, lose their patience, and write from abroad: "A nation that can not make its own clothing, its bunting for its flags, and carry its own letters, deserves to be placed where foreigners place us—between the Russians and Negroes in point of civilization." And in the face of all this living testimony of all nations, Mr. HELPER indifferently takes up his dark-lantern, and, negrofied all over, exclaims: "Slavery! Slavery!" And our poor laborers, still suffering from the dreadful crisis and general insecurity, listen with mingled feelings of hope and fear to the false prophet.

National independence, diversity of employment, work for every talent, consolidation of our settlements, humanity to our laborers, humanity to the laborers of the world, real, solid, undisturbed, steady progress; all point us to a home market, to home industry, to a home policy, to home protection, recommended by all our statesmen, from WASHINGTON, JEFFERSON, and MADISON, to JACKSON, CLAY, and WEBSTER, while the party tricksters and mistaken philanthropists have, these long years, mystified the different interests of the people with the question of Slavery, as if it were the sole point wherein the nation was sore and suffering.

It is not our present purpose to adduce extensive facts and reasonings on the subject of the harmony of the different interests. We only ask our countrymen whether we might not, with equal propriety, use, at least to a considerable extent, Mr. HELPER's language about the South, in reference to our whole Union. Substituting "Europe" for "the North," who can fail to be struck with the adaptedness of his language to our whole common country—to the Slave States and to the Free States?

"*Europe* is the Mecca of our merchants, and to it they must, and do, make two pilgrimages per annum—one in the spring and one in the fall. In one way or another, we are more or less subservient to *Europe* every day of our lives. In infancy we are swaddled in *European* muslin; in childhood we are humored with *European* gewgaws; in youth we are instructed out of Northern books [by teachers who have learned from European volumes, we may add]; at the age of maturity we sow our 'wild oats' on *European* soil; in middle life we exhaust our wealth, energies, and talents in the dishonorable vocation of entailing our dependence on our children, and on our children's children, and to the neglect of our own interests and the interests of those around us, in giving aid and succor to every department of *European* power; in the decline of life we remedy our eyesight with *European* spectacles, and support our infirmities with *European* canes; in old age we are drugged with Northern physic [that may be so to some extent]; and finally, when we die, our inanimate bodies, shrouded in Northern cambric [or rather in *European* broadcloth], are stretched upon a bier, borne to the grave in a Northern carriage, entombed with a Northern spade [by an *Irish* grave-digger], and memorized with a *European* slab!"

So we go! There is bathos for you! This is what somebody calls an inverted climax, or the art of sinking! Mr. HELPER followed his man up, or rather down, to the very grave, than which there is nothing lower! As we are sadly deficient in that sort of genius, his language came to us much *à propos*. A peroration characteristic of this subject of exhaustion!

XIII.—THE FIRST CAUSE AND LAST EFFECT.

In all his hosts of numbers and numerical deductions, Mr. HINTON ROWAN HELPER has forgotten one great agent; namely, Population — the very beginning from which every number and show-table comes, and the very end in which they all must concentrate again—the very original cause and the very ultimate effect—the fundamental basis and the crowning top of the whole industrial edifice, with all its manifold figures, Arabic and Roman.

We will start with a few facts or principles, the most of which are self-evident. Whenever there is any explanation needed, we will give it, still as concisely as possible in order not to interrupt the general train of our argument.

XIV.—POPULATION THE FUNDAMENTAL CAUSE OF PRODUCTION.

Production depends upon Population. Where there is not the latter, the former can not be. The larger the population is, the more extensive must be production, at least in our civilized communities. Generally one hundred men can produce more than fifty can. And, indeed, production not only keeps pace with population, but even goes ahead of it.

This question is of too great importance to be lightly passed over. For there were those, and probably are still some, who believe that a curse rests upon all increase of population. Men came to this belief especially from the fact that certain nations of modern ages could no longer support their inhabitants, who therefore were forced to leave their homes and to seek subsistence in countries as yet more thinly settled. Philosophers have been very busy trying to find a cause and a law for this phenomenon. The English economist, MALTHUS, at last thought he had found them. "Population," he says, "tends to outgrow the production of food; Population increases in a geometrical progression, while Production increases only in an arithmetical one." This theory is in immediate connection with that of RICARDO in regard to the course of cultivation, namely, "that society begins with cultivating the most fertile soils, and, as population increases, must take possession of the poorer and less productive ones." According to this compound theory, Production grows more slowly than Population. A nation must thus continually expect smaller returns for the labor of its inhabitants; they have less to consume, less to live upon, and poverty and misery must be the end. SISMONDI, one of this school of economists, uses, in this respect, the following precious words: "As soon as population has increased to too large an extent, that is, as soon as over-population takes place, the surplus must yield to a dire necessity. The earth must swallow again the children she can not nourish." Providence must thus take refuge in pestilence and war, and thus decimate human society at proper times; else over-population will take place, with all its horrors of poverty and starvation. According to this theory, the human race has the great privilege of choosing between two evils—war and murder, or famine and starvation, with some slight variation of pestilence, or expatriation to a country where the doom, however, is only delayed for a while.

Let us cast away this direful irony on Nature and Providence! These learned commentators on the plans of God have misinterpreted the story of Pandora's box. Hope is still left to man, and left to him until "he enters hell." Nature is not so gloomy as their theory, and poor Providence, too indulgent, must not too often bear the complaint of friend and foe. RICARDO's hypothesis, on which, to a great extent, the whole bloody theory is based, has been found entirely false. Men have everywhere, as H. C. CAREY has proved, begun with the cultivation of the higher and less productive soils, and descended gradually to the lower and more fertile ones, to cultivate which the first settlers had not the requisite capital. But even without this, knowledge, and capital, and production must necessarily increase with the increase of population. We will not further discuss this point, but add some statistical proofs from the "Testimony of the Nations."

McCULLOCH says about England: "The population of England, since the eighteenth century, has doubled; the production certainly tripled or quadrupled."

PEUCHET, one of the most celebrated statisticians of Europe, says: "The peasant in France, who formerly had known but very gross food and unhealthy beverage, has now meat, wine, bread, and beer. If we turn to Germany, the change for the better is still more striking than in France; and thus, while the numbers of the population are continually increasing, their comforts and enjoyments are increasing still more rapidly."

A writer in one of the agricultural journals of Bavaria, after a most careful examination and statistical comparison, says: "The present emigration from Europe is not commanded by necessity. Europe itself is an agricultural continent. The present population is 263,000,000. If order and quiet would reign, 400,000,000 of people might easily be supported." The southeastern part of Russia might alone feed a whole continent.

Production increases, then, faster than population. That this is the case with the United States, too, writers of every description have proved, by filling their volumes with pleasing tables concerning the great increase of our material happiness.

We do not wish to be misunderstood in this. We said, that it is population which causes the production and originates thus the statistical show-tables of exports and imports, of agriculture and commerce, and of every item of national wealth and happiness which can be expressed by numbers. We went further, even, and showed that a hundred persons produce not only twice as much as fifty, but even more; perhaps three or four times as much—for different reasons to state which we will not interrupt our general argument. And this is the opening of *our* labyrinth! But we will go slowly, and may, at our pleasure, safely retrace our steps.

XV.—RATIO OF INCREASE OF POPULATION IN DIFFERENT COUNTRIES.

We know now, on the whole, the effect of population on production. Now let us compare the statistics of our own country with those of other leading nations of modern civilization, and see at what rate nations generally increase in population! Let us find out whether we, the United States of America, are above or below the common rate. We will *not now* ask why or wherefore, but only see and compare the statistical facts. Their connected thread will gradually lead us to causes and influences which worked upon Mr. H.'s show-tables of the South and of the North.

TABLE VII.—RATIO OF NATURAL INCREASE OF POPULATION OF DIFFERENT COUNTRIES COMPARED WITH THE U. S.

[*From the Census of the U. S.*, 1850.]

States.	Year.	Population.	Year.	Population.
Great Britain,	1800	15,800,000	1851	27,475,000
England	1801	8,350,000	1851	16,921,000
Ireland	1805	5,395,000	1851	6,515,000
Scotland	1801	1,608,000	1851	2,888,000
France	1801	27,349,000	1851	35,783,000
Prussia	1816	10,349,000	1849	16,331,000

		1800		1851
	Whites	4,304,000		19,553,000
	Fr. Col'd	108,000		434,000
United States	Slaves	893,000		3,204,000
	Total	5,305,000		23,191,000

We will add here the table which shows the increase of the population of the United States from decennium to decennium.

TABLE VIII.—RATIO OF THE INCREASE OF THE POPULATION OF THE UNITED STATES FROM DECADE TO DECADE.

Years.	Whites.	Free Colored.	Slaves.	Total.
1790	3,172,000	59,000	697,000	3,929,000
1800	4,304,000	108,000	893,000	5,305,000
1810	5,862,000	186,000	1,191,000	7,239,000
1820	7,861,000	238,000	1,538,000	9,638,000
1830	10,537,000	319,000	2,009,000	12,866,000
1840	14,195,000	386,000	2,487,000	17,069,000
1850	19,553,000	434,000	3,204,000	23,191,000

We see from these tables that Great Britain has not quite doubled its population in fifty years. England, separately or with Scotland, has a little more than doubled in the same number of years. France has, during that same half century, increased its numbers by only a little more than one half, and Prussia has, during that time, increased at about the same rate as England. To double the population in about fifty years, has been the highest ratio obtained by any of these modern nations, though some statisticians state that England doubled its population in forty-five years. Or, as the Census says: "The annual increase of the United States has been nearly three times as great as that of Prussia, notwithstanding the large population that was added to her by the partition of Poland; more than four times as much as Russia; six times as much as Great Britain; nine times as much as Austria; ten times as much as France."

But how does it come that the United States is so much ahead of any other nation? During the same fifty years it has increased its population to almost five times its original number. It has not doubled in fifty years, but in twenty-five, nay, almost in twenty, if we compare only the white tables.

Everybody will, of course, give IMMIGRATION as the reason of this extraordinary increase. But let us see how much this faster increase of our population is due to immigration.

XVI.—RATIO OF THE NATURAL AND ARTIFICIAL INCREASE OF THE POPULATION OF THE UNITED STATES.

Should we proud Republicans, modern Israelites, and modern Romans—as we are often called—measure ourselves and our natural productiveness by the standard of other nations, such as England, France, or Prussia—called the most enlightened nations of old Europe—our numbers would, at best, have doubled in fifty years; that is, our population would have been, in 1850, 10,610,000, instead of 23,191,000. There would remain an increase of 12,581,000 which could not be accounted for otherwise than by immigration. Or, if we take only the white population, there would have been, in 1850, 8,608,000, instead of 19,553,000, and the immigrants and their descendants would then be 10,945,000.

Let us see another account. An able statistical writer,

from Washington, who took great pains in his calculations, arrived, after having carefully counted each year's increase, at the following conclusions:

ABLE IX —THE NATIVE WHITE POPULATI N
[*From Hunt's Merchants' Magazine, No. CXCVI.*]

The native white population of the United States, in 1850,
would have been, without immigration since 1800..... 8,995,000
    "   "   "   " 1810..... 10,710,000
    "   "   "   " 1820..... 12,318,000
    "   "   "   " 1830..... 14,330,000
    "   "   "   " 1840..... 16,771,000
And the *immigrants and their descendants* number, in 1850,
since 1840... 3,265,000
" 1830... 5,656,000
" 1820... 8,669,000
" 1810... 9,277,000
" 1800... 11,032,000

One account ascribes thus to immigration, since 1800, 12,581,000; the other, 10,945,000; and the third account gives 11,032,000.

What right have we, now, to reject one of these accounts or an approximate number? Do we procreate more children than other nations? Is our ratio of annual births over deaths more favorable? Do we live longer? And if some statisticians wish to have it so, have they ever given full weight to the effects of immigration on the tables of population? If they give the ratio of our natural increase as being 0.13 or 0.30 per cent. in our favor, may they not have been slightly mistaken in their difficult calculations? Did they know, and if so, did they make due allowances for the fact, that children of foreign parents, though born but one day after their mother's arrival on this soil, are all classed among the natives? But though the result of our numerical and ethnological comparisons and deductions can hardly be doubted, still we will fortify it by another consideration: namely—the fact that the immigrants increase naturally faster than the natives, and, therefore, help proportionately more than the natives to fill the tables of population. We quote from a speech of the author, delivered some years ago at Albany:

"This fact," he says, "has but lately attracted public attention. In the Massachusetts census of 1855, the reporter, summing up his statistics, finds that the native population of that State is about three and a half times larger than the foreign one, but that the births are almost equal, 48 per cent. native, and 46 per cent. foreign, the rest unknown. He looks with wonderment at those numbers, and comes to the conclusion that the immigrants must propagate themselves quicker than the natives. Foreign women, he calculates, must produce children three times faster than American ladies. Yet this greater fecundity of foreign women is not confirmed, certainly not to that extent. Newspapers came, then, to the aid of the perplexed reporter, and stated that there were more foreign females in Massachusetts than males; but this also did not explain the proportion of the increase. The reporter remains puzzled, and he guesses, at last, that if that increase goes on at the same ratio, the foreigners will yet swallow the natives.

"Now, this mystery is fully explained by our above observation, namely, the *great proportion of grown-up persons among the immigrants*. This is the fundamental cause of the faster increase. Take on an average an equal number of foreigners and natives, and there will be more grown-up persons among the foreigners, and therefore more marriages, and then more children. Many foreigners in that number will be ready to enter the vineyard of the Lord, and extend the empire of human flesh, while as many natives are yet lying in their nurses' arms, with hardly flesh enough for their own tender limbs."

But let us see the proportion of grown persons among the immigrants. We refer to the table of Mr. EDMUND FLAGG, the efficient Superintendent of the Statistical Bureau of the State Department. It is for the year 1855, but may well be taken as a standard for former years, for the proportion of grown persons must in those times have been still larger, as it is but lately that immigrants have had the confidence to come, with their whole families, to this "far-off land."

TABLE X.—THE AGE OF IMMIGRANTS.

[*From the Report of the Superintendent of the Statistical Bureau of the State Department*, 1855.]

Age.	Males.	Females.	Total.
Under 5 years of age	8,000	8,000	16,000
Between 5 and 10 years	7,000	6,000	14,000
" 10 " 15 "	6,000	5,000	11,000
" 15 " 20 "	8,000	16,000	34,000
" 20 " 25 "	24,000	16,000	40,000
" 25 " 30 "	22,000	10,000	32,000
" 30 " 35 "	13,000	5,000	19,000
" 35 " 40 "	9,000	4,000	12,000
Forty years and upward	12,000	7,000	19,000
Age not stated	11,000	8,000	19,000
Total	135,000	89,000	224,000

This table shows that three fourths of the immigrants may be taken as persons between the ages of fifteen and forty-five. Now, set these two classes of new-comers in our nation at work—on one hand you have the products of natural increase by birth, on the other the products of artificial increase by immigration;—the former nothing but frail little children, to be petted and nursed for years to come; 75 per cent. of the latter commonly stout and healthy, and at once ready to work and produce;—the former yet exposed to all those decimations by the diseases and dangers of the young; the others, already tried and decimated on land and sea, and only those of them counted who had stood the trial ! Now, let this process go on year after year, which will increase proportionately faster?

But we will be liberal toward ourselves! We will not take the twelve millions, or the eleven millions. We will, on account of the somewhat greater mortality of foreign children, go still a million or so lower, and say that about one half of the white population of the United States in 1850 is due to the immigrants and their descendants since the year 1800.

[According to the well-known statistician, F. H. BRACHELLI, the number of inhabitants of German origin, in 1856, was 5,250,000, viz., about the fifth of the then population of the United States. If we now add to this number of Germans the large Irish immigration, and then that of the other nations of Europe, our own account will be found rather too low than too high.]

And if, then, it is true that about one half of the white population of the United States is due to the immigrants and their descendants since 1800, would it not be a fair conclusion, too, that the statistical show-tables of "material" products—and such are most of those expressed by numbers—owe at least half their swellings to the immigrants? Which class of inhabitants are chiefly engaged in "material" production? We may be allowed to quote once again from an address of the author:

"Certainly, this Union might have reached its present power—I do not say without immigration at all (for we are all immigrants), but without immigration since 1800—but not so soon, not so fast; it would have had to toil and to grow yet many years to come. There would now be less capital here, less cultivated land, less commerce; there would be fewer engines, fewer shops, fewer roads, fewer vessels, fewer houses and palaces, fewer comforts, and fewer luxuries. Your men-of-war, your fortifications, your public buildings, your power at home, your power abroad throughout the world, your private and public treasuries would dwindle, and many of the natives who are now managers, and conductors, and directors, and merchants, and speculators, and officers, and reverends, and doctors, and judges, and senators, most honorable Senators, many of them, would now be common day-laborers, mechanics, instructors, or canal diggers—professions which are most graciously left to the foreigner—professions of less honor, of less pay, but of more labor."

The same language may be observed in the columns of the New York *Tribune* (March 11, 1859):

"Our able and ambitious youth are attracted to trade, to the professions, to fillibustering of some sort—rarely to any form of productive industry. Advertise to-day for a man to manage a farm, and three fourths of the responses will come from men of *European* birth. Advertise for a boy in a lawyer's office, a clerk in a store, a partner in a venture to Pike's Peak, and two thirds of the responses will come from *native Americans*. We are, as a people, intent on getting suddenly rich by some kind of speculation, rather than on slowly acquiring a competence by industry."

Thus, should the above number of the foreigners and their descendants be found even somewhat too large, there would be no doubt about our final conclusion, that at least one half of the common production of the country is due to them.

XVII.—RATIO OF IMMIGRATION IN THE DIFFERENT STATES OF THE UNION.

We have thus seen how much of the population and how much of its more rapid increase, how much of the production and how much of its larger tables, must be due to immigration. We now will ascertain what portion of this immigration fell to the part of the South, and how much to the part of the North, and then we will try to find the causes of the difference.

We take again the Census of the United States for 1850. There we will see the proportion of foreigners—"not born here"—to the natives, "born here, whether from native or foreign parents." For the official census is liberal toward the children created abroad but born here; they are all called "natives." Our tables, however, do not suffer in this case, since all States are treated alike liberally.

[We expressly give our statistical tables in round numbers, in order to impress more strongly their general character, and the proportion of their difference when compared with one another.]

TABLE XI.—THE RATIO OF FOREIGNERS IN THE FREE STATES.

[*From the Official Census of the United States*, 1850.]

Free States.	Total Inhabitants.	Foreigners.
California	92,000	21,000
Connecticut	370,000	38,000
Illinois	851,000	111,000
Indiana	988,000	55,000
Iowa	192,000	20,000
Maine	583,000	31,000
Massachusetts	994,000	163,000
Michigan	397,000	54,000
New Hampshire	317,000	14,000
New Jersey	489,000	59,000
New York	3,092,000	655,000
Ohio	1,980,000	218,000
Pennsylvania	2,311,000	303,000
Rhode Island	147,000	23,000
Vermont	314,000	33,000
Wisconsin	305,000	110,000
Total	13,434,000	1,908,000

THE RATIO OF FOREIGNERS IN THE SLAVE STATES.

Slave States.	Total Inhabitants.	Foreigners.
Alabama	771,000	7,000
Arkansas	209,000	1,000
Delaware	92,000	5,000
Florida	87,000	2,000
Georgia	906,000	6,000
Kentucky	982,000	31,000
Louisiana	517,000	67,000
Maryland	583,000	51,000
Mississippi	606,000	4,000
Missouri	682,000	76,000
North Carolina	869,000	2,000
South Carolina	668,000	8,000
Tennessee	1,002,000	5,000
Texas	212,000	17,000
Virginia	1,421,000	22,000
Total	9,612,000	304,000

XVIII.—CAUSE OF THE DIFFERENCE IN THE PROPORTION OF IMMIGRANTS IN THE DIFFERENT STATES OF THE UNION.

During our whole argument we heard frequent whispers of: "Slavery! all due to Slavery!" We will now make some "excerpts" from the above statistical tables, in order to see whether those whispers were oraculous.

THE NUMBERS.

TABLE XII.—DIFFERENCE IN THE PROPORTION OF IMMIGRANTS IN FREE STATES.

States.	Square Miles	Foreigners.
New York	47,000	665,000
Pennsylvania	46,000	303,000
Massachusetts	7,000	163,000
Vermont	8,000	33,000
New Hampshire	8,000	14,000
Wisconsin	53,000	110,000
Michigan	56,000	54,000

TABLE XIII.—DIFFERENCE IN THE PROPORTION OF IMMIGRANTS IN SLAVE STATES.

States.	Square Miles.	Foreigners.
South Carolina	28,000	8,000
Georgia	58,000	6,000
Kentucky	37,000	31,000
Louisiana	41,000	67,000
Tennessee	44,000	5,000
Florida	59,000	2,000
Alabama	50,000	7,000

TABLE XIV.—DIFFERENCE IN THE PROPORTION OF IMMIGRANTS IN SLAVE AND FREE STATES COMPARED.

States.	Square Miles.	Foreigners.
Maryland (Slave)	11,000	51,000
Maine (Free)	35,000	31,000
Louisiana (Slave)	41,000	67,000
Iowa (Free)	50,000	20,000
California (Free)	188,000	21,000
Missouri (Slave)	65,000	76,000
Michigan (Free)	56,000	54,000

TABLE XV.—SOME ADDITIONAL DIFFERENCES IRRESPECTIVE OF SQUARE MILES.

Free States.		Free and Slave States.	
States.	Foreigners.	States.	Foreigners.
Connecticut	38,000	Mississippi (Slave)	76,000
Rhode Island	23,000	Iowa (Free)	20,000
Massachusetts	163,000	Maryland (Slave)	51,000
Illinois	111,000	Vermont (Free)	33,000
New Jersey	59,000	New Hampshire (Free)	14,000
Wisconsin	710,000	Kentucky (Slave)	31,000
Indiana	55,000	Maine (Free)	31,000

There are four tables as simple as the multiplication table. In the *first* of them there are seven Free States. In none of these is there any Negro Slavery. Why, then, is there such a difference in their share of immigrants? New York and Pennsylvania have about the same number of square miles; but the former has about twice as many immigrants. Vermont and New Hampshire, too, have about the same area; but the former, again, has over one half more foreigners than the latter. Massachusetts, with about 1,000 square miles less than either, has still more than ten times as many foreigners as the one, and five times as many as the other. Wisconsin, with about the same number of square miles as Michigan, has more than twice as many foreigners. Has Southern Negro Slavery exerted its whimsical influence even on the Northern States?

But look at the *second* table. There, again, are seven States. All Slave States! And still, South Carolina, with an area half that of Georgia, has one fourth more immigrants. Louisiana has only one seventh more square miles than Kentucky, and still has more than double the number of immigrants. It has fewer square miles than Tennessee, but twelve times as many foreigners. Florida and Alabama have about the same area, but the latter has two thirds more foreigners. What is the reason of this difference? Negro Slavery again? Is Negro Slavery blacker in Florida than in Alabama? Is the Negro less a Negro in Louisiana than in Tennessee?

Let us pass on to the *third* table. Another seven States, some Free, some Slave. There is Maryland with its Slavery, and Maine with its Freedom. And still Maryland, with only one third of the area of Maine, has 20,000 more immigrants. Louisiana has one fifth less square miles than Iowa, and still the Slave State has three times as many foreign inhabitants as the Free. California, with more than four times as many square miles as Louisiana, has three times less foreigners. Missouri, with one seventh more square miles than Michigan, has two sevenths more foreigners. Has, in these cases, Negro Slavery been an attractive force?

Or, let us take Northern and Southern States without reference to square miles, as in the *fourth* table; for there is, both South and North, plenty of room for a hundred times more immigrants. Has Negro Slavery caused Connecticut to have more foreign inhabitants than Rhode Island? Massachusetts more than Illinois or New Jersey? Wisconsin more than Indiana? Mississippi more than Iowa? Maryland more than Vermont or New Hampshire? Kentucky the same number as Maine?

Or, compare the number of foreigners in each State with its native population; or the number of foreigners to the square mile with all the inhabitants to the square mile; the different States will most stubbornly resist a common rule or law, but especially will they object to such quack barometers as the *deus ex machina* invented by Mr. HINTON ROWAN HELPER.

From the facts and numbers presented by us, any impartial reader must see that there were other causes at work besides Slavery to direct the waves of emigration, and to produce such a difference in the numbers of foreigners in the different States. From the earliest period of our Union, the emigrants have chosen certain ports, which were not pointed out to them by the white or black color of some of the inhabitants, but by the great order of Nature. Places like Boston, New York, Philadelphia, Baltimore, or New Orleans were the great and tried harbors to receive the emigrants. They were the great starting-points selected by Nature as the principal thoroughfares of the Western Continent. Many of the emigrants, then, when once arrived on the shores of their "Promised Land," would not, could not, wander far into the interior, and only a small minority went out of the regular course to States and places on the left or on the right.

As the inland routes were gradually opened, they moved in larger numbers farther to the West. This was in accordance with the country's policy, which, on the whole, was to scatter the population over an area as large as possible, to form new Territories and new States, to get new agricultural products to exchange for foreign fabrics, instead of building up the home market, and consolidating and developing the old lands and States. But when the emigrants saw their plans thwarted in the East, and new hopes and "free homesteads" held out in more distant regions, whither should they move? Neither was cotton the article of growth which they were acquainted with, nor had the South the climate which they were accustomed to in the countries from which most of them came. They, therefore, went North and West! Says the celebrated statistician, G. F. KOLB: "It is the climate similar to that of Central Europe which attracts the emigrants to the *North and West* of the United States, in preference to any other land." We add here a table which shows which climate sends the most emigrants, and which might thus expect the most:

TABLE XVI.—PLACES OF BIRTH OF THE FOREIGN POPULATION OF THE UNITED STATES.

[*From the Census of the United States*, 1850.]

STATES.	Number.	STATES.	Number.
England	278,000	Austria	900
Ireland	961,000	Russia	1,000
Scotland	70,000	Norway	12,000
Wales	29,000	Denmark	1,000
Germany	573,000	Sweden	3,000
Belgium	1,000	Prussia	10,000
Holland	9,000	British America	147,000
Switzerland	13,000		
Total			2,116,000

2,116,200 emigrants come from the Northern and Middle States of Europe, and the total number is only 2,212,000 ! How many remain to be counted to the southern parts of the world ? France, Italy, Spain, Greece, Mexico, and the whole of Asia, have only about 90,000 to be divided among them.

There is, then, the climate, the geographical position, the river-beds, the bays and the harbors, the lakes, the mountains and valleys, the soils and the zones, and many other natural facts, which determined the future of this whole continent and of the different States long before the first foot of civilized man touched this soil. The Tiber and the Thames, the Nile and the Rhine, had their histories predicted by the Book of Nature long before a Rome or a London, before pyramids or castles, were dreamt of. And so the St. Lawrences, the Hudsons, and the Mississippis of this continent had their future marked out long before Mr. HELPER came, trying to negrofy our understandings.

XIX.—EFFECT OF IMMIGRATION ON THE SHOW-TABLES OF THE SOUTH AND OF THE NORTH.

Let us now sum up this whole matter of immigration. We have stated and proved that population is the fundamental cause of all production ;

That if the population increases, the production must increase at a still higher ratio ; or that, if there are twice as many persons at work, they will " manufacture" thrice or four times as large and as plentiful show-tables of every sort and material ;

That population in our land increases at a most enormous rate, and that neither England nor France can keep up with it ;

That this extra glory is, however, not due to any natural privilege, but to the immigrants, of whom seventy-five per cent. are, like Melchisedek, already grown up when they are born; or—what is the same for all practical considerations—when they are borne to this country;

That at least one half of the population of the United States in 1850 is due to the immigrants and their descendants since 1800;

That the different States, whether Free or Slave, had different proportions of these immigrants;

That this difference can not be explained alone by Mr. Helper's universal cause of everything under creation: namely, Negro Slavery;

That nature has marked out the course of empires, and that Providence does not first make cities and then rivers to flow by them, and at last shores and banks to keep *them* in proper limits.

And now, if we take another look at the tables we have presented, we see that the whole number of foreigners—foreign-born inhabitants—in these United States is 2,212,000, of which the Free States take about six sevenths, and the Slave States only one seventh.

If, now, we take this as a general ratio—and we may, according to other tables, fairly do so—of the whole immigration and descendants since 1800, and call this whole immigration only 10,000,000, we find that 8,500,000 of these artificial helps were allotted to the North, while the South received only 1,500,000.

Now, set two countries, or two sections of a country, at work, the one receiving annually a fresh supply of men and women at the rate of 7,000 to every 1,000 of the other—continue this process for a period of fifty years, these foreign men and women continually digging and toiling, producing matter and men with eagerness, increasing in numbers at rates so astonishing, cultivating lands, working day, and even night, in the sweat of their faces, with bodies stout and hands accustomed to labor, bringing millions of dollars into the country, saving old and laying up new stock, increasing and thriving lustily on a fresh and grateful soil, in a free land, in the very midst of industrial progress, in an era to which none previous in history can be compared as to swiftness of production and effective means and instruments to assist the hand of man—let these proportions (seven to one), under such most favorable circumstances, and under influences never dreamed of before, work on for a period of fifty years—add then to this, if you please, the difference between the Northern and the Southern laborer—take the Negro as he is, wholly barbarous, half barbarous, or half civilized, unskillful at least, for many years, causing for a long period a heavy draft on Southern treasure for the purchase-money (mostly paid to Northern traders)—a slave, too, and, as such, ready and willing to work only because and when he must—a slave *now*, to be a slave forever, as far as he knows, without hope of position or of gain; while the immigrant brings, at least, traces of the civilization of the world with him, is a free man, works for himself, appropriates whatever wages he may make and whatever his wife and children may earn—the master of his hands, of his family, of his property, with considerable chances for honor and position even—let the two sections under such different influences work on for a period of fifty years, and at the end of this period compare the numbers and figures, the statistical tables of wealth and of products, of commerce, agriculture, and manufactures of the one section and the other, aside from all the various natural causes favorable to the one and disadvantageous to the other—will you be surprised to find the tables of the one much lower than those of the other?

We are not surprised that the statistical tables of the North are so much larger than those of the South, but we are surprised that they are as large in the South as they *are*. The South has done more than we should have expected, under existing circumstances.

But, let none imagine that should the South at once liberate all its slaves, there would be such a rush of immigrants as Mr. HELPER would like to see, by the aid of his dark-lantern. It will take many generations to accustom the Northern-born native, or foreigner, to more Southern climes, and only a slow and steady advance will, or can, give the South the artificial aid which will enable it to increase more rapidly in numbers and men. And this slow and steady advance, as far as destined by Nature, has been going on this long time, in spite of Negro Slavery, which, to be sure, has lessened the pressure, but could not stem the flood. But that rush of foreigners can not, even in the North, always remain the same. It has probably reached its crisis. It will, and does sink, and in the same manner the Northern show-tables will and do sink, while the South, less accustomed to artificial aid, will feel less the growing want. There is not total darkness in the future of the South! Let it manage its powers well! Let it give a willing ear to the teachings of history! Perhaps DE SOTO's dreams about the Valley of the Mississippi may yet be realized, and in that great central empire of the continent of North America, the South "will not be the least among the children of Israel."

XX.—THE ULTIMATE EFFECT OF PRODUCTION ON POPULATION.

It is a question, after all, whether the greater amount of production in a country is a sure index of a corresponding degree of happiness and welfare among its people. Already the Italian economist, Fuoco, said: "Not production, but distribution, is the first and principal question in economy."

And BLANQUI, in his "History of Political Economy," called this same idea "the great motto of the social science of the nineteenth century."

One nation may, indeed, produce a vast amount of material products, and still keep the producers, especially the laborers, in a miserable condition, by giving them but a small share in the common produce. Another nation with a smaller amount of products may distribute this amount more equally and proportionately, and thereby procure a greater amount of common happiness. Just as in the case of families. One father may gain twice the amount that another does, but use proportionately six times as much to gratify his own selfish appetites. The family of the latter will be the better off; there will be a greater amount of happiness caused by a smaller amount of means. In a nation, the fathers with the depraved appetites are the rich and privileged squanderers. The whole principle may be stated thus: A nation is well off, not in proportion to the amount, but to the equal distribution and the rational use of its wealth and products—a field as yet little explored by the science of statistics!

Without now going further into an elaborate discussion and explanation of this question, however important it may be, we will merely state that the natural increase of a people, their quality remaining unimpaired, is generally taken as an index of the degree of their happiness. But we repeat, this increase shows less the amount of the production of wealth, than the proportion of its distribution. The principle itself, however, is unassailable in its general bearing.

We now apply this to the population of the South.

XI—THE NEGRO MULTIPLYING—*HIS* SHOW-TABLES ALL RIGHT.

We will compare the Negroes under different masters. H. C. CAREY, in his work, "The Slave Trade, Domestic and Foreign," Chapter II., shows that in all the British Islands where there was Negro Slavery, the Slaves universally decreased in number. He first takes up Jamaica, and shows that the number of Negroes imported into that island can not have been less than 700,000. "If to these," he continues, "we were to add the children that must have been born on that island in the long period of 178 years, and then to reflect that all who remained for emancipation amounted to only 311,000, we should find ourselves forced to the conclusion that Slavery was here attended with a destruction of life without a parallel in the history of any civilzed nation." In St. Vincent, the births steadily diminished in number. In British Guiana, there was a decrease of 12,000 from 77,000 in fifteen years! and a similar decrease in other colonial possessions. The number emancipated in the West Indies was 660,000, while the number imported and retained for home consumption had certainly amounted to 1,700,000.

Had Mr. HELPER known this, or spoken of it, how "the chevaliers of the lash, and the robbers and the murderers," would have again flown from his lips! But let us see what the statesman and economist CAREY says, who has certainly as much philanthropy as the showman, HELPER:

"While thus exhibiting the terrific waste of life in the British Colonies, it is not intended either to assert or deny any voluntary severity on the part of the land-holders. They were, themselves, as will hereafter be shown, to a great extent, the *slaves of circumstances, over which they had no control*, and it can not be doubted that much, very much, of the responsibility must rest on other shoulders!"

This is the same H. C. CAREY whom Mr. HELPER brings up among his Testimonies of Living Witnesses! Might there not, in the South of our country, too, some such extenuating circumstances have been found which should have tempered somewhat Mr. H.'s wrath and bridled his bloody tongue? We will see!

Mr. CAREY passes on to Negro Slavery in the Union, and after a most careful examination and comparison of statistical tables, gives us what he calls "a tolerable approximation to the number of Slaves imported into the territory now constituting the Union, namely, on the whole, 333,500."

"The number," he says, "now in the Union exceeds 3,800,000; and even if we estimate the import as high as 380,000, we then have more than ten for one; whereas in the British Islands we can find not more than two for five, and perhaps even not more than one for three. Had the Slaves of the latter been as well fed, clothed, lodged, and otherwise cared for, as were those of these Provinces and States, their numbers would have reached seventeen or twenty millions. Had the blacks among the people of these States experienced the same treatment as did their fellows of the islands, we should now have among us less than one hundred and fifty thousand Slaves!"

Has not Mr. HELPER been "too hasty in making up his mind on the subject," though he says the contrary? Has he not "jumped at conclusions," though he denies it? Has he acted with "perfect calmness and deliberation," as he so naively asserts? He says, that "the non-slaveholding white of the *second* degree of Slavery is treated by the slaveholders as if he were a loathsome beast." How must the Negro of the *first* degree of Slavery have been treated? Who or what stands a degree lower than "a loathsome beast?" Mr. HELPER's dictionary of Vile Words not being at hand, the question must remain unanswered for the present.

And still, the Negro lived, his cheeks grew fat, his body plump, he multiplied and replenished the earth, and we have seen as jolly a crowd of darkies down in Richmond, as ever on Boston Common or in the Wilds of Africa!

Now, who tells a falsehood, Mr. HELPER or his Numbers? It is the old story again! The Numbers are all well. But Mr. H. sees "through a glass darkly."

XXII.—EVERYBODY LIVING LONGER THERE WHERE THE "NIGGERS" ARE.

Those Southerners, in spite of their Negro Slavery, have still produced *some*thing. They have, as Mr. HELPER indirectly proves, *some* agriculture, *some* manufacture, *some* cotton, *some* banks, *some* railroads; they write, or at least send, through the post-office *some* letters, found *some* schools and libraries, publish *some* newspapers, give *some* votes, build *some* churches, get out *some* patents, *some* Bibles and *some* tracts, harbor *some* foreigners, send out *some* missionaries, and do *some*thing for colonization and civilization. But not only this: we find at the end that these people " down South" do, after all, not suffer a great deal from their producing only *some* rye, and *some* wheat, and *some* newspapers, and *some* lot cabbage, for: *They do not only not die faster than the Northern people, but, on the contrary, they are healthier and live longer.* We add a table to prove:

TABLE XVII.—RATIO OF DEATHS TO LIVING POPULATION.

[*From the Official Compendium of Mr. Helper's Crisis.*]

MOTTO OF HIS TITLE-PAGE.—"The liberal deviseth liberal things, and by liberal things shall he stand."—*Isaiah.*

States.	Percentage.
Southern States (Slave)	1 in 74.60
Northern States (Free)	1 in 72.39

TABLE XVIII.—AMERICAN LONGEVITY.

[*From a recent edition of Blake's Biographical Dictionary.*]

States.	Number of Deceased Centenarians.
Southern States (Slave)	68
Northern States (Free)	59

The reason for this greater Mortality and shorter Longevity in the Northern States must lie somewhere hidden among "the Potatoes, the Clover-Seeds, the Brood Mares, the Beans and Peas, the Stall-fed Beef, and other Produce," from which Mr. HELPER so scientifically draws his arguments.

Now, which is the better of the two? To produce fast and die fast, or to produce slower and live longer? Of what use is all our digging out, and heaping up, and gathering in, when during all the trouble necessary in this process of production and reproduction, our heads grow light, our hearts gloomy, and our bodies lank, and at the end of the whole *affaire*, when at last the time for enjoyment should have arrived, Pale Death comes to give us kindly the last stroke, that sends us beyond the reach of the dunghills of our material wealth?

While the reader is left for a moment to himself to decide which part to choose, we will gather up whatever is left of Mr. H.'s statistical existence.

XXIII.—THE POSTERIOR PART OF MR. HELPER'S STATISTICAL BODY.

The main body of Mr. H.'s statistics is contained in that part of his Compendium which precedes the Dead and Living Testimony. We are through with that. There remains now nothing but the Appendix, which, by-the-by, has all the characteristics of appendixes in general. It is protracted, unmeaning, and winds up in a curl.

There is a whole sea of mysterious numbers, all carefully labeled with "Negro Slavery," and any amount of Northern gewgaws, strewn around like Yankee notions, interspersed with sundry rhetorical flourishes " excerped" and repeated from the Body of his Statistics. It is a kind of deluge after the Testimony of the " Wiser and Better" men.

But, unconsciously or with his wonted impartiality, Mr. HELPER puts, at times, some seasoning in, which makes the surface a little more palatable. Such is his innocent slur on the number-filled North. To be sure, he does not spare the Southern " breeder, buyer, and seller of bipedal black cattle, who withal professes to be a Christian," but he speaks also of " Northern quacks, Northern lashes for

Southern slaves, Northern gimcracks and haberdashery." This is quite a relief. But the Northern pianos, Northern knives, and Northern apparel are carefully repeated. We at first thought, in seeing these old faces again: "Here beginneth the second" edition of the same book!

But the most attractive part in this appendix of several chapters, is the grand display of Mr. HELPER's logic, unassisted by the dark-lantern. For it must not be expected that he again brings forth but *one* reason—namely, his old cherished Negro Slavery. Not at all! The appendix hangs rather loose from the body and plays its capers with wanton individuality.

We will now give the curious reader a few examples of that caudal logic:

He says that the South has contributed but little to the cause of Negro Slavery in Kansas, and the reason of it is, not Negro Slavery this time, but the poverty and the niggardliness of the Southerners. This *exceptio in principiis* would be admissible were it not for the delicacy of its terminology.

In his chapter on offices, he proves that the Southerners have, in most cases, the majority, all on account of Negro Slavery; but when he accidentally finds an office where the Northerners happen to have the majority, he does not give Negro Slavery as the reason, but superior or special talent which can only be grown up North. (Mr. HELPER is from North Carolina.)

He shows, then, the comparative literary character of the North and of the South, by giving the number of newspapers, and especially the circulation of the New York *Tribune* and the New York *Herald* in the Free and Slave States. We think, of course, highly of the newspaper, but that would be stretching its influence *ultra modum et decorum.*

He also measured the physical and mental activity of the members of the United States Senate, by the number of public documents they frank. According to this calculation, CHANDLER, of Michigan, has over twenty times as much of that article as CRITTENDEN, from Kentucky. And DOUGLAS, of Illinois, has three hundred times as much as SUMNER, of Massachusetts. "This shows, also," Mr. H. says, "that the people of the South are not a reading people; but tobacco, politics, and especially fine-looking wenches, constitute the warp and woof of their conversation." Mr. DOUGLAS sent 345,000 documents, that is, more than all the Free States Senators together (Mr. CHANDLER excepted). He is not one of "the lazy pro-slavery officials," we suppose, "who perpetuate the ignorance and degradation of their constitutents."

He complains that he was not able to publish *his* book in the South, when he had just given extracts from the Charleston *Standard*, which in strong terms criticised the condition of the South. This is called by logicians a *contradictio in adjecto.*

He thinks, too, that the city which publishes the most books and papers must, *eo ipso*, be also the most literary. Poor "country folks," like Mr. HELPER and his reviewer, must renounce their fame to the glory of New York, Boston, or Philadelphia. And then he adds, that the executors and agents of CALHOUN, BENTON, SIMMS, and other Southern writers, send their works to be published in New York. The reason for this strange phenomenon is Negro Slavery, and, therefore, all right!

These examples are all nicely set up in copious numbers, and surrounded with occasional whinings, such as about the poor women working in the field, whom he would like to advance into the frying-pans of factories.

But at last he proves that the non-slaveholding whites are very illiterate, and thus, we humbly think, that they can not read, much less understand, his book! Now, this crowns the whole! Poor Mr. HELPER can neither reach his subject nor his object. He is no agitator! He only addresses the non-slaveholding whites, and for them he wrote his book! and, now, on the very last pages of his volume, he proves that his clients can not read! Why did he not first write a "Webster's Spelling-Book" for the non-slaveholding whites of the South?

And thus he winds himself through, until, on the last page, in "indignation and disgust" over what he wrote, he curls up in the following graceful style:

"*Southern Literature is a travesty on the profession of letters*," and "*Southern Religion is a stench in the nostrils of Christendom.*"

Negro-nursed Washington! first son of the South and of the Union! ward off the heartless curses of a perverted man, whose motive may be good, but whose tongue runs loose and wild. There is now a dearth of great men, North and South! Send us whole-souled men, no matter what zone or section may produce them! We do not need, as yet, "American Platos, Homers, Shakspeares, and Humboldts," but send us a few more Statesmen, who, dispassionate but unflinching in their principles, are able to lead our great empire safely through the storms that overhang it!

XXIV.—CONCLUSION.

We think we have thus proved, in this Book, that the famous Numbers, or, in other words, the Statistical Disparities between the Free and the Slave States, do not justify our resorting to violent words and violent measures, whereby we increase the enmity between the two sections, and make the Union appear less desirable and less honorable.

They give us no reason why we should be ashamed of the South, and throw heartless curses on its land and people.

But we must here abstain from any general remarks on the great question. In this first Book we have strictly confined ourselves to the Numbers; in the second, we will treat, in a similar way, the Testimonies. After having, then, overthrown these two *separate* arguments, we will face the *whole* question.

BOOK II.

THE TESTIMONIES.

BOOK II.

THE TESTIMONIES.

IN REPLY TO CHAPTERS II., III., IV., V., VI., VII., AND VIII.
OF MR. HELPER'S COMPENDIUM.

I.—SINGLE TESTIMONIES.

WE will now show that the *Testimonies of single men and nations, taken from their historical connections*, have no better claim than the Numbers.

Were we to follow separate testimonies, we would forever be tossed around as on a stormy sea, knowing not whither to go. But there is a steady progress of humanity—a progress which gradually corrects or overrides all individual fancies and theories, and teaches us, in the plastic forms of real events, the ways and measures for our future course.

But before we lay before the reader the mark-stones of this progress, and give Slavery its relative place therein, we will first pass in review the Testimonies as they are presented by Mr. HELPER. We take *him* again, because he has classified them better than any one before him. We may seemingly aid Mr. O'CONOR, but we do this only in order to overthrow, once for all, that double-faced sophistry which draws its arguments from single and disconnected Testimonies.

II.—THE CHAPTERS III. TO IX. OF MR. HELPER'S COMPENDIUM.

At the beginning of Chapter III., Mr. HELPER advises the people "to forget for a moment what he has written on the subject of Slavery, and to ignore all that he may write hereafter." Though it be difficult for us to forget or to ignore what he has not yet said, the object of the advice is highly commendable. For, after having given his own opinion, he now appeals to the "sayings of wiser and better men," to collect which has cost him "much time, labor, and money." Our indebted country has probably, by this time, repaid him amply for his trouble. Trouble it must, indeed, have been to collect such an array of opinions, and all of them well assorted, in Mr. HELPER's style—first Southern Testimony, then Northern, afterward the Testimony of the Nations, then that of the Churches, three pages of Bible Testimony, and, at last, thirty pages of Living Witnesses to bring up the rear! A formidable array, forsooth! But though his course differs sadly from that which he promises in his introductory chapter, where he says, "It is not our purpose to draw a broad line of distinction between right and wrong, to point out the propriety of morality and its advantages over immorality, nor to waste time in pressing a universally-admitted truism, that virtue is preferable to vice," still we take his issue, and put these abstract opinions in their proper light. Should we, perhaps, at times, throw too much shadow upon the picture, we must be excused; for Mr. HELPER, has certainly been too light, and airy, and spiritual in *this* part of the work. Wherever his heavy and dark brush appears, we will not fail to supply the necessary light.

III.—THE TESTIMONY OF THE UNION.

Mr. HELPER seems, at first, to know the way we ought to follow. But when we think ourselves near the longed-for aim, we perceive that he, like an *ignis fatuus*, has led us astray. We seem, indeed, to be in duty bound, in these moments of danger, to wander religiously to the graves of our noble forefathers who have made us one and united, and to seek at their shrine light and knowlege for our fear-beset ways. But when, with HELPER's help, we are at the sacred spot hallowed by the memories of common struggles and the time-honored compact of our Union, what does Mr. H. show us? Naught but mangled bones, torn with sacrilegious hand from venerable bodies! For such are his "excerpts" and "extracts."

We can not and we will not deny the noble sentiments of the founders of our republic. We know that Freedom, in the abstract, finds more sympathizers among the great and noble of this world, than Tyranny and Slavery. We know that our forefathers, almost to a man, thought our Slavery to be an evil, and we honor them for it. But did they ever use such language as Mr. HELPER? Did they ever propose such schemes and measures? He has shown in what respect our common forefathers *agreed* with his own sentiments, why did he not show, too, in what they *disagreed* with him? WASHINGTON, "the father of our country," an example to us in all that is really good and great—though he had such ardent wishes for the gradual abolition of Slavery, what measures did *he* propose? What plans did *he* favor? Or, was LAFAYETTE's scheme, in form or spirit, anything like that of our modern philanthropist? Or, was FRANKLIN's Society for Promoting the

Abolition of Slavery anything like that corporation of Non-Conformists which he proposes among the non-slaveholding whites of the South? Or, where are the rebellious harangues of JEFFERSON, who yet called the Slaves "citizens and brethren?" Where the great stratagems and proposals of MADISON, who yet opposed the introduction of the term "Slave" or "Slavery" into the Constitution? Or, has Mr. HELPER more greatness of soul than WASHINGTON, more stern republicanism than JEFFERSON, more wisdom than FRANKLIN, or more virtue then MADISON? Or, take the representative men of a second generation! Are the WEBSTERS, the CLAYS, knaves and fools compared with him? Has it not been, heretofore, a well-understood principle among all the statesmen of our republic, to look upon Slavery as upon an *undeniable historical fact*, whatever our *abstract opinions* may be about its right or wrong? And, is this course of action of our noble ancestors not as certain, not as frank, not as important as their abstract opinions? Was it not always their policy, instead of putting forth their opinions about Slavery, rather to think of means and ways to get along with it, and to harmonize, as far as it was possible, Union and Reform? In all their endeavors to abolish Slavery, did they not always carefully appeal to the slaveholders themselves, and this, indeed, privately, and not through the organs of an excited populace? And did all those great men of other times—our foremost pride, our greatest honor in the eyes of the world—did they, by suppressing over and over again the temptings of their "abstract opinions," and by continually contriving new ways of peaceful reform, did they, the noblest men of our entire history, by yielding thus, defame their character or pollute their manhood?

There never fell from their unstained lips, words like these:

"Peevish,—Sulky,—Mean,—Boors of Vandalic hearts and minds, —Irreverent Distorters of the Truth,— Savage, Barbarous Kidnappers,— Chevaliers of the Lash and Lords of the Shackle!"

Are these, words of a friend and brother? Are they words of an enemy, even? Are they words of a man? Or, have the insulted shades of our common forefathers already smitten the intemperate one with insanity? These are not words to soothe! These are not the means to heal! This is not the language of Peace and Union!

IV.—THE TESTIMONY OF ENGLAND.

Mr. Helper is an unrelenting foe. His collective industry is inexhaustible. He is not content with appealing to our own noble ancestors. After having "excerped" testimony in favor of his opinion from the wise men of the South and of the North of his own land, he introduces, or uses in a similar way, the Testimony of the Nations. He begins with England. Now, we do not think that Locke, Fox, Pitt, and Burke would have acted more nobly, more liberally, and more prudently than Washington, Franklin, Hamilton, and Webster, if they had been placed in similar circumstances. But still, we can not and will not question England's philanthropy.

To be sure, the condition of depopulated Ireland is still pitiful to behold. Says a recent writer on Ireland: "An Irishman has nothing national about him except his rags." Or another: "Let an Englishman exchange his bread and beer, and beef and mutton, for no breakfast, for a lukewarm lumper at dinner, and no supper. With such diet, how much better is he than an Irishman?—a Celt, as he calls him. No, the truth is, that the misery of Ireland is not from the human nature that grows there—it is from England's perverse legislation, past and present." Or, let us look at our own shores! How often we find the brave and warlike Celt of former days, crippled and degraded by ages of tyranny and oppression! But, England is philanthropic, and the Irish are not Negroes, nor are they Slaves!

Or, let us turn our eyes away from Ireland across the ocean, toward that happy land of emancipation. Says a recent writer: "A short term and cupidity strain the lash over the poor Coolie, and he dies; is secreted if he lives, and advantage taken of his ignorance for extended time when once merged in plantation-service, where investigation can be avoided." But again, the Coolies are no Slaves; they are but hired servants, and England's philanthropy is safe!

We are not yet through with the Testimony of England, who is always loudest in condemning our Slavery. We will give her a fair hearing. How closely she watches those poor Hindoos! How effectually she keeps them down, whenever they express any dissatisfaction with the happiness she forces upon them! She has instituted among those "half-naked barbarians" an awful *solidarité*, by which the province is responsible for the labor of all its men and women. But still, England is philanthropic! She has carried rails and Bibles, free-schools and steamboats, telegraphs and libraries to India, all for the benefit of those half-naked barbarians! And should telegraphs and Bibles not have the requisite effect of happifying, opium will be administered to them, and to "all the world, and to the rest of mankind." She will no longer permit those savage Hindoos to roast as witches wrinkled old women, for she knows too well, from her own experience, the unfairness of such proceedings; nor does she, in these days, allow anywhere the Hand of Justice to cut the ears of those who speak against State or Church. Now, this is decided progress! England is the civilizer and Christianizer of the world! To be sure, there is still robbing and flogging, murdering and starving enough in the "dominions of the Gracious Queen, where the sun never setteth;" but England, nevertheless, dislikes Slavery in general, and Negro Slavery in the United States in particular, and her lords and ladies are ever ready to eat and drink with the poor commoners of the West, eager of philanthropic royalty! There are similar laurels waiting for Mr. HELPER, and we are glad, for his sake and our own, that he has appealed to the Testimony of our Cousins!

But England emancipated her slaves in the West India Islands! She expended £20,000,000, we suppose, from sheer philanthropy, and may we ask: Whom did her philanthropic measure benefit? Jamaica, that brilliant island, saw her land and people degenerate, says H. C. CAREY; the planter sold cheaply and left, the slave did not work. Such must be the effect of all revolutionary or sudden abolition; and, though the emancipated lands may gradually recover from the ill-devised blow, they can only do so with loss of much property and at the cost of much human misery.

V.—THE TESTIMONY OF FRANCE.

After England comes France, as usual. But this Testimony comes at rather a peculiar time. Not many years, or even months, ago, France was concerting a plan to introduce "voluntary Negro labor" into her tropical colonies, the demand for whose products was so rapidly increasing everywhere. It was said that England herself, at first, had favored the plan, but after having looked somewhat deeper into the scheme, her philanthropy, or some other hidden virtue, got frightened, and she dissuaded her noble ally from accomplishing the voluntary Slave-trade. For, what was it but a second edition of the Slave-trade, perhaps in some improved style, *à la Française* or *à la Coolie?*

But Mr. HELPER speaks of ROUSSEAU and MONTESQUIEU! Does he think that the "constitutional" MONTESQUIEU would have acted differently from our "constitutional" MADISON? Or, did LAFAYETTE act differently from JEFFERSON, the renowned pupil of ROUSSEAU and VOLTAIRE? But, then, has Mr. H. any idea of the gloomy age in which those philosophers lived and wrote? There were in that century thirty-seven famines, more or less severe, in France. ROUSSEAU wrote his *Contrat Social* to starving millions, and MONTESQUIEU's *Esprit des Lois* was but a futile remedy for a dying generation. Alas! what misery was brooding at that time, unheeded, by the side of reckless extravagance! France was approaching her revolutionary crisis! But the blood of a hundred thousand, slain on the altar of Liberty, could not wash away her tyranny! And the blood of other hundreds of thousands, slain to the idol of Glory, could not wash away her crimes! And in the face of this self-condemnation, Mr. HELPER brings up the Testimony of France! Let France sweep at her own doors! There is, as yet, as much dust and dirt in her precincts, as there was in the twelve stables of AUGIAS!

VI.—THE TESTIMONY OF GERMANY.

Germany, thou famous land of thought and theory! Where are thy radical statesmen, to teach us systems like those of Mr. HELPER? Thou land of slow movements, thou land of forty tyrants *ex officio*, and forty hundred times forty hundred assistant masters with pens and lashes, with anathemas and jails! Oh, unfortunate collector! More unfortunate still in your individual citations!

We pass by the aristocratic GOETHE, who, in his love of humanity, had scarcely time to think a moment of his country's weal or woe, and venture a few remarks on LUTHER, better known in this land.

We must be aware that the people of LUTHER's time, like our own "good folks," were not eager after reforms in matters of religion only. In their articles of demands, the religious and worldly elements were always mixed and blended with each other. "Priests chosen by the community," they asked for, and "No more Serfdom;" "Freedom of Belief—and Abolition of unjust Taxes." The spiritual and temporal always went together. And they had reason enough to think of *this* world also; for, "they were badly clothed, dwelt in houses without floors or pavements, slept on straw, lived on 'black' bread, apples, and water, saw meat but rarely, and many never at all, and had often no bread, even."

The conservative NIEBUHR, even, had to confess that the right was, at first, on the side of the poor people. But how did LUTHER feel and act toward the despairing wretches? When he heard about their rebellion, he wrote: "Let the balls fly among them; else they do still worse things. There is no need of pity. Obey they must! God, surely, will save the innocent, as He did Jeremiah and Lot. If He does not, they surely are not innocent!" Rather harsh language! Or, in his letter to Baron EINSIEDELN, who had asked him whether he should liberate his slaves: "The common man," he answered, "must be loaded with burdens, else he will grow too wanton." And loaded and burdened he was! The revenge taken on those poor peasants was horrible. Those who had saved their lives and fled home to their families were hunted out and cruelly murdered or blinded, mutilated, and disgraced. Barefooted were they forced to beg forgiveness from the hand of their oppressors, and fines were laid upon them, to pay which it took generations and generations. LUTHER, even, was at last moved to pity; for, "cruelty seemed to have gone too far."

But this would lead us beyond the limits of our present undertaking. We only think that Mr. HELPER could hardly have made good Abolitionists of LUTHER and GOETHE.

VII.—THE TESTIMONY OF RUSSIA.

Mr. HINTON ROWAN HELPER does not know much of the political condition of the Russian people, we suspect. The privileged noblemen themselves are not very free. Says a Russian: "Their privileges are, to take office *if* they can get any; to leave it *when* they are dismissed; to go abroad *if* they get passports; and to buy real estate *if* they have money." And these are the "upper-ten" of Russia. There are, then, some twenty or thirty classes of other subjects, partly slaves and partly free, and wholly unfree and completely slaves, amounting to an indefinite number of millions. Among them, there is a continuous emancipation, in the Russian sense of the word, and the most modern *coup d'état* of ALEXANDER III. is not without precedents among the former Alexanders. It is a difficult thing to emancipate those people of thirty or forty different races and of as many different customs, duties, and languages; and a wholesale emancipation, though sounded with the roaring voice of the Northern Bear, is a sheer impossibility. Nor does the present emperor mean it so, though Mr. HELPER may have read his *ukas* so. Moreover, if the emancipation is to be intrusted to the same worthy officials who had the supervision of oppression and taxation, then woe to the new-made Russian freeman! He will have to pay dearly for what *they* call liberty. So much for the Home Department. Now a word about Foreign Affairs.

We do not generally take Russia as a model of freedom, nor do we expect much from her in this line. Nor does she herself much believe in the liberty of the races. She has helped Austria in subduing Hungary, and has just finished a hundred years' war against Circassia. The last Will of PETER the Great is her Bible, and her Czar is her God. Freedom can be hoped for only as far as it does not conflict with the one or the other. The prospects of liberty are, then, not very fair, and we think even a Russian edition of the " Compendium of the Crisis" would change matters but little.

VIII.—THE TESTIMONY OF GREECE AND ROME.

This Testimony is simply absurd; for one needs not to be a scholar to know the theories and practices of Greece and Rome in regard to Slavery. Slavery was a fixed and acknowledged institution among all the states of antiquity.

They went still further. XENOPHON calls *all* manual occupations dishonorable and unworthy of a citizen. PLATO says that such occupations degrade those who exercise them. SOLON, the oil-merchant, made some allowances for the trader only, probably from an *esprit de corps*. ARISTOTLE calls the slave a part of the family property. That good old philosopher has some ugly passages, which do not savor much of Abolitionism. "Nature herself," says he, "has made Slavery," and he reasons thus on it: "The *animals* (man included) are divided into male and female. The male is more perfect, and therefore commands. The female is less perfect, and thus obeys!" (ARISTOTLE does not seem to be very sound on the *Punctum Xanthippicum*, or Women's Rights question.) "But, well," continues the philosopher, "there are among men those who stand as much below others as the body below the soul, or the beast below man. And these individuals, fit for physical labor only and incapable of doing anything more perfect, are destined by Nature for Slavery, because there is nothing better for them than to obey. But what great difference is there, after all, between a slave and a beast?" Singular Abolition doctrines these!

Yet one glance at Rome. JUVENAL says: "The Romans consume the nations to their very bones." They had temples erected to JUPITER, the Plunderer, and disliked commerce, "because it has made others their slaves." But why should we waste time about something which schoolboys can teach? Mr. HELPER, the Blunderer, alone can quote such examples from History! The domain of antiquity and classical antiquarianism belongs entirely to Mynheer VAN DYKE and to your Honor Mr. O'CONOR.

IX.—THE TESTIMONY OF THE CHURCHES AND OF THE BIBLE.

Mr. HELPER writes two chapters on this subject. But we think the Churches—or, rather, Mr. H.'s clergymen—may just as well be omitted. For they either teach the Bible, on which all churches are more or less based—in which case they are superfluous—or they do not teach what the Bible does, and then Mr. H. must have already included them under his "wiser and better men" of each nation and section.

But our collector has again stepped on dangerous ground. We will quote for him a few verses from the Old and a few from the New Laws. He must try to get along with them the best he can.

We read in Leviticus xxv. 44, 45, 46: "Both thy bondmen, and thy bondmaids, which thou shalt have, shall be of the heathen that are round about you; of them shall ye buy bondmen and bondmaids. Moreover, of the children of the strangers that do sojourn among you, of them shall ye buy, and of their families that are with you, which they begat in your land; and they shall be your possession. And ye shall take them as an inheritance for your children after you, to inherit them for a possession; they shall be your bondmen forever: but over your brethren the children of Israel, ye shall not rule one over another with rigor."

In 1 Timothy vi. 1, 2 we read: "Let as many servants as are under the yoke count their own masters worthy of all honor, that the name of God and his doctrine be not blasphemed."

The venerable THOMAS SCOTT adds, in his "Commentaries on the Holy Bible," in the one case: "The Israelites were thus permitted to keep slaves of other nations." And in the other case: "This shows that Christian masters were not required to set their slaves at liberty."

Now, we are generally called a Christian nation, and are often compared to the Israelites of old. But neither in the one character nor in the other are we forbidden to keep slaves, nor could we as a Joint Stock Company of Christian Israelites derive, in any way, such a prohibition.

But why refer to a book—and especially now—which has been used, and turned, and interpreted, and falsified in so many different ways, to serve any sect, or party, or fancy, or ambition in the history of social tyranny and freedom? Why refer to a book whose "Kingdom is not of this earth, but of the Life to come?"

Let us never mention it in settling or discussing our Slavery question! There is inflammatory matter enough between us! We do not want to call still more the *odium theologicum*, that most odious of church-feelings, to our aid! We are a progressing humanity! Our heavenly wants may, in all these phases of development, remain the same! The forms of worship, even, may be unchanged! But our *worldly* wants certainly *do* change, and with them the forms of social and political life. Therefore, let the Bible no more interfere, lest we put the Good Book into a false position.

X.—THE TESTIMONY OF LIVING WITNESSES.

We are now, happily, over the opinions of the "wiser and better men," and are prepared to judge upon the Testimony of the Living Witnesses. Thirty long pages of Living Witnesses! A formidable phalanx, which Mr.

HELPER might—as he says—increase *ad infinitum*. Now, we do not undervalue the testimonies he has thus collected, nor even those which he might have collected, or may yet collect in times to come. Nor yet do, or can we refute them as they are. They are all very good in their proper places. But one thing pleased us considerably, namely, the fact of such a motley crowd of Living Witnesses all being thrown pell-mell on one and the same platform. SEWARD and SNODGRASS, SUMNER and PHILLIPS, GERRIT SMITH and BURLINGAME, CAREY and PARKER, GREELEY and RAYMOND, BEECHER and BELLOWS, CHASE and TAPPAN, and forty or fifty others, all huddled together in one common group! Has any human mortal ever seen such a number of so different characters brought together so peacefully on any previous thirty pages of cotemporary history? No, not in a directory, even! They all have nearly the same opinions about Slavery in the abstract, but how different are their actions! Some of them act just as WASHINGTON or JEFFERSON did. But there are others whose consciences require, in addition, the establishment of Underground Railroads; others, again, may be called practical men, they use the abstractions as party capital; there is a class, too, who, being of the catholic cast, think—"Faith without works is dead!" and therefore furnish pikes and money for others to battle and to die in the cause of human liberty; there is, indeed, a small number—abstract opinions always being equal—who really fight, and fear neither death nor the gallows; there is also quite a number who think most bravely, but "take it out" in talking, and some few go even further than the rest, and try to induce the Negroes to rise in rebellion against their masters, and achieve, with blood and murder, their inborn African liberties! And all these different characters stand on Mr. HELPER's pages firmly knit together! Must these Living Witnesses not be surprised at the company they are forced to keep? At any natural occasion of contact, they would fly to the four winds on discovering such neighbors as Mr. H. gives them! But what humanity and patriotism could not do, Mr. HELPER's jugglery has accomplished. They are all in apparent harmony. This is certainly a "curiosity in literature."

XI.—GENERAL REMARKS ON THE TESTIMONIES.

These are the Testimonies. We did not add to each class of them their counterparts, which might easily have been found in the History of Opinions, or might have been gleaned, without much trouble, from the writings of the Pro-Slavery apostles, but we confined ourselves to a few illustrations. What is true of them, is true with respect to all others which the HELPERS and the O'CONORS may, jointly or separately, with limited or unlimited responsibility, hereafter collect and classify. By reasoning from single opinions, or even from single facts, we may at our pleasure successfully prove or disprove the same thing.

We are, in this connection, spontaneously reminded of the famous dialecticians of old Greece. They were masters in casuistry, and they knew that they were when they went to Rome to display their power. There they disproved, before astonished crowds, in the afternoon, what they had proved in the morning, and carried conviction at both times. The Roman people were at that time but little skilled in rhetorical tactics, and they applauded altogether too liberally. Such is the popular heart, often yielding too generously to momentary impressions. *Tout comme chez nous!* Such arguments are, therefore, very useful on occasions when momentary excitement is all that is aimed for. But they are valueless when we want a sound and solid basis for our course of action.

But before taking leave entirely of Mr. HELPER, we will yet look a moment at the bloody Plan with which Numbers and Testimonies, collectively, have inspired him. It is a proposal for a wondrous *coup d'état*, which would at once rid us of all our difficulties.

XII.—MR. HELPER'S BLOODY PLAN.

Long before Mr. H.'s great chapter on Abolition arrives, its approach is perceived by the more intemperate rhetoric. The beginning of the chapter itself is, however, in quite a humorous and pleasant strain. It is like the deceitful smile of sunshine while the thunder-clouds are already towering over the hills that gird the horizon. So *we* take it, at least. "The non-slaveholding whites," says Mr. H., " ought to demand from the slaveholders any number of millions of dollars for the decrease in value of their (the non-slaveholders) lands, during the dark period of Slavery in the South." Well, these non-slaveholding whites might just as well protest against their having been born, and sue their parents for the damages sustained thereby. For, their fathers or grandfathers, or somebody higher up in that transcendental line that leads to ADAM, must be responsible for those brawny "members from Africa," who are the cause of all the mischief. But Mr. H. must intend this whole compensation matter merely for fun; else he would not, shortly after, have adduced testimony to prove " that the non-slaveholders possess the poorest lands, and the slaveholders own the most fertile soils." We let it, therefore, pass as a little fun, and will look again into the angry face of the threatening storm-cloud.

Like distant thunder, the famous Plan for Abolishing Slavery gradually draws nearer. It has an ugly look at the outset, and seems to promise hard weather. Some excuses, pressed out by an overburdened conscience, fall like rain-drops through the sky. But the thunder-cloud is unrelenting. Nearer and nearer it draws, until at last it stands, mad and roaring, over our heads, and, raging, unfurls its blood-red banner of Destruction and Desolation.

" 1st. Thorough Organization and Independent Political Action on the part of the Non-Slaveholding Whites.

" 2d. Ineligibility of Pro-Slavery Politicians—Never any other Vote to any one who Advocates the Retention and Perpetuation of Human Slavery.

" 3d. No Co-operation with Pro-Slavery Politicians—No Fellowship with them in Religion—No Affiliation with them in Society.

" 4th. No Patronage to Pro-Slavery Merchants—No Guestship in Slave-waiting Hotels—No Fees to Pro-Slavery Lawyers—No Employment of Pro-Slavery Physicians—No Audience to Pro-Slavery Parsons.

" 5th. No more Hiring of Slaves by Non-Slaveholders.

" 6th. Abrupt Discontinuance of Subscription to Pro-Slavery Newspapers.

" 7th. The Greatest Possible Encouragement to Free White Labor."

A few rain-drops, sprinkling excuses on the BOTTSES and STANLEYS, BROWNS and BLAIRS, proved that the storm had passed away. Some more little thundering in the distance, and all was over. The sky was clear, the sun shone bright, and nobody was hurt, " frankly, fairly, squarely."

But, earnestly, has anybody ever seen more moonshine and madness put into the sacred Number VII. ? What a horrible and ridiculous heptade ! what an awful slaughter-house platform ! what a septuple nonsense ! And all this language Mr. H. addresses to the non-slaveholding whites, " who are," as he says, " cajoled into the notion that they are the freest, happiest, and most intelligent people in the world, and believe what the slaveholder tells them." Mr. HELPER addresses this murderous heptalogue to these " illiterate" non-slaveholding whites, " who are but one step in advance of the Indians of the forest, who are deplorably ignorant, three fourths of the adults not being able to read or to write their own names" [the other fourth being probably comprised in the flattering term " white sycophants who have negroes around"]. Now, add to this such language as—" Haughty cavaliers of shackles and handcuffs, and lords of the lash," while the Northerners are the " liberty-loving patriots," then you have all the elementary ingredients, not of a common Abolitionist of old NOAH's or WEBSTER's stamp, but of the HELPER caste, " whose line of duty is clearly defined, and whose intention it is to follow it faithfully or DIE in the attempt."

Now, we humbly think that in Kansas, at Harper's Ferry, and in Charleston, there have been shooting and murdering, hanging and dying, enough. We do not exactly mean by this to dissuade Mr. HELPER altogether from dying, if he thinks he would help the cause more by his death; but still we believe that for "common folks," and for the great majority of people in general, it would be better "to do one's duty faithfully" and LIVE in the attempt. But in order to work *and* live, a different plan is needed from that of Mr. HELPER. His is, indeed, a *dying* effort, scented with the cold air of the grave and the unfriendly fragrance of corpses.

We attempt to oppose to this war, blood, and death scheme, a Living Plan—a work of friendship and peace, a proposal of union and harmony, not drawn from the heated crucible of our own individual fancies, hopes, and passions, but from the great workshop of nature, which lies open to all faithful students of history. It may not be covered with the smiles of sunshine and the pleasing light of flattered prejudices, but it leads not to perpetual war and final destruction.

BOOK III.

THE DEVELOPMENT.

BOOK III.

THE DEVELOPMENT.

I.—SLAVERY IN HISTORY.

LET us smother for a moment the angry feelings which long disputes have aroused within us; let us lay aside all artificial issues to which enmity and exasperation have forced us; let us ignore all arguments and theories which ambition, self-interest, and pride have created; let us forget all hostile acts, on one side and on the other, to which our blind passions and false issues and arguments have carried us; let us then look at Slavery as it appears in History, not from the narrow platform of American party politics, but from the broad family circle of humanity, of which our nation is a member. Let us *cast away all polemical spirit* and look at Slavery objectively as a historical fact, and trace it back in the different periods of the Story of Man, so that we may see its development and divine from the Past the prospects of the Future; for this is the spirit in which we must study History.

We will, however, not give a learned treatise, but only sketch its course, until we arrive at our own doors, and see our own Slavery and the circumstances which surround it.

Though the generous minds of the whole civilized world

may deem it inhuman in *principle* for a man to own his fellow-man, still History, on all its pages, declares itself decidedly in favor of the *fact*. From the remotest ages, man has been owned and Slavery has existed, though names and forms may have differed. War seems to have been everywhere the origin of it—at least, in the earlier stages of human society—just as war was then the sum total of all international intercourse. If, in civilized ages, war is the exception—or, at least, ought to be—and peace the rule, so, in barbarous periods, war is the rule and peace the exception. In these struggles of barbarous tribes, the prisoners of war were considered the property of the victors, who held this property by no common law, but by force. The victors held unlimited authority over their prisoners; they could destroy or keep them, just as any other kind of property which had in some way become their own. In times or cases in which these live prisoners were of no use, they were killed; and they were *not* killed only when they could serve the victors to some purpose, in which latter case they became slaves. This is the origin of Slavery in the times of barbarism of any nation or tribe—in the primitive phases of human society, where "Might is Right." The slave himself had his right to become free whenever there was not enough might or force to keep him longer in subjection.

The *word* "slave" is of modern origin, as it first appeared in the long struggles between the *Slavonic* tribes of the East and the Western Europeans of Germanic origin, in which the former were generally overcome and subdued.

Let us now see how it has been with Slavery in the nations and ages which have heretofore claimed some right to the title of civilization. There have, as yet, been but three great civilizations in the world : the old Asiatic, in its manifold branches, the Greco-Roman, and the Modern European, in which latter, also, this continent, as a great European colony, must be reckoned. In the two former civilizations, that is, among the so-called ancient nations, Slavery was a *conditio sine qua non*—the fundamental condition of their system of social economy. It was the great characteristic of all ancient national compacts, and wherever we cast our eyes we find it. It came to them from the times of their barbarism, and was sustained and increased by many accidental causes in their history. It was a punishment for crime at one time, a payment for debt at another. It was the last disgrace to which the gambler was to submit among some nations; it was the last means to shield the poor and weak from hunger and danger among others.

But as these nations advanced in culture and civilization, the condition of the slaves became modified. They were still the principal laborers in all the branches of rising industry (for "man" seemed not to have been made for labor, but only for war and the chase, and labor was only worthy of a slave, of a low-bred man, or, in some nations, of woman); but they were treated more gently, and obtained some rights and privileges. Though these nations never abolished Slavery entirely, still we know the friendly intercourse between master and slave, especially among the Greeks and the Romans. Thus, could the slave, among the Athenians, sue his master for cruel treatment. Beating a slave or killing him was reserved to the public authorities. A slave was allowed to gain and to own property, and to buy his liberty. Similar was the condition of the slave in the Roman Empire. Though the Justinian Code still granted to the master the *vitæ necisque potestas*—the right to pummel and to slay—still the whole tenet had become obsolete in practice. The master was often satisfied with a certain tithe or daily payment, as is the case in our own Southern cities, and he frequently promised his slave entire freedom as soon as he (the slave) had gathered a certain amount of property. There were many manumissions for various other causes, such as extraordinary fidelity, or self-sacrificing services of any kind. Slavery must, indeed, have changed considerably in character, since even most skillful artists and men of superior education and refinement were found in its ranks, and great poets, generals, and statesmen were born in Slavery, or of slave parents.

Modern civilization may be said to have begun with the appearance of the Germanic nations upon the theater of Europe, especially since the time of the overthrow of the Western Roman Empire. As long as they were in a barbarous or semi-civilized state, they obtained and held slaves in the same manner as other tribes and nations. During the eighth, ninth, and tenth centuries, even, there were, according to the best authorities, as many slaves in Germany as there were free men. Among the Anglo-Saxons, the per-centage of slaves was even still greater. But in the Slavery of the different modern nations that rose on the ruins of the old Roman Empire, similar changes took place, as in Greece and Rome. The sale of slaves to a foreign land was forbidden at an early time, and their general condition, mostly by reason of the influence of the Christian Church, was gradually so much improved that it deserved even another name. The slave,

THE DEVELOPMENT. 85

during the so-called period of chivalry and feudalism, became a "serf," and Slavery became serfdom, not unlike the Roman colonate in the latter times of the empire. The serf was less owned as to his life than as to his service. Serfdom may thus be regarded as the great stepping-stone to freedom, just as, *vice versa*, the poor free man, in those feudal times, often sank to the state of serfdom. We do not mean by this that Slavery was changed into serfdom by a positive law. But that intermediate and mitigated condition of the Slave was none the less a reality. Thus, in England, " Villany" originally meant Slavery; but it was a different thing in the middle ages.

This, again, was similar in Rome and modern Europe. But there the Romans stopped. This milder form of Slavery continued as long as the empire itself, and even survived its fall. This was not so with the modern nations. There arose, in spite of old systems and old theories, a new element, a new principle, with the advance of industry. It was "Honor to Labor," the characteristic element of the triumphant civilization of the modern nations. It is this principle which prolongs the lives of modern empires, and will finally bring about the civilization of the world. It is the *want* of this principle which brought decay upon the ancient nations before the foot of the barbarian had even yet trodden upon their soil. It is " Honor to Labor" which brought the man of labor at last to honor and freedom. Gradually his burdens grew less. Instead of all the labor of his whole day, the serf owed only part of his labor to his master, and then only certain services at certain seasons or in certain contingencies. What formerly was unrewarded service, gratuitously demanded and offered, received some remuneration, though small it may have been. Such remunerations became, with the increased productiveness of labor and the increased value of the laborer himself, more adequate, until forced service became voluntary service, since the lord held up as high rewards or wages for labor as any other person. These are some of the ways in which serfdom passed away, though the extinction of its last forms required some legislative enactment. Such enactments were made in most nations of Europe during the seventeenth and eighteenth centuries; and after many ages of struggles, the enslaved man became at last free.

II.—NEGRO SLAVERY IN HISTORY.

Negro Slavery is as old as any other Slavery, and its origin is war, as among any other tribes, nations, or races, be they white, yellow, or red. Prisoners of war were slain or made slaves, in the continent of Africa, long before European and American slave-traders appeared on its shores—long before BARTH, the learned traveler, saw black slaves owned by black masters—long before the interests of African industry "tied the Negroes to the plows and drove them like oxen."

Among modern nations, the Spaniards were the first who made and owned African slaves. It was during their long wars with the Moors or Arabs, who, in their western stream, had spread over the whole northern part of Africa, even to the Pyrenean Peninsula, and had taken, for many centuries, a firm footing on Spanish soil, at the very dawn of modern European civilization. During these struggles and wars with the Mohammedan intruders of Asia, who once threatened to subdue all Europe, the Spaniards at last drove them away to Africa, and followed them in their turn to that continent. The wars continued there, and the so-called "Black Moors," the real Africans by birth and race, had often to expiate for the wrongs committed by the "Arabian Moors."

But after the discovery of America, when the *Industrial* Period of Modern Civilization began, this kind of Slavery, namely, Negro Slavery, changed radically its character. While among all nations, in China even, and on all continents, Slavery became milder, and was slowly passing from every country where there were but the faintest rays of civilization, Negro Slavery took a new and powerful start. Let us view, a moment, the relative position of this fact in the history of the world's progress.

The continent of Africa, the land of the Negro—if we take Negro as the general term for those manifold tribes that inhabit Africa—was the last which appeared on the great theater of the civilization of the world.

ASIA had its time the first of all the continents. It was the cradle of human progress. It had grown, lived, and decayed, before our present nations and their civilization, their lands and continents even, were dreamed of. Their social life was, indeed, confined to one continent, and on this continent, again, the Chinese were separated by insurmountable barriers from the land and civilization of the Hindoos, and these again from the civilization of Western Asia, which itself stretched only to the Mediterranean and its shores. Egypt was but a small part of Africa, and may as well be counted to Asia, and the Phenicians and Carthagenians pierced but little into the continent of Africa. The great Sahara was the Western and Southern limit of their empires. Thus the Asiatic colonies on the one side, and the young rising kingdoms of Media and

Persia on the other, extended but little the area of this civilization, which remained truly Asiatic in origin, form, and character.

Then came the GRECO-ROMAN civilization. This, too, stretched, in spite of its extensive wars and glorious achievements, over only a comparatively small area, in which the shores of the Mediterranean and the adjacent lands were, and played the principal parts. We know, indeed, that the great empire of Rome, in its period of highest splendor, stretched over the *totus orbis terrarum*— over the whole world; but we know, too, how large this "whole world" was—with no America, with almost no Africa, with little of Asia, and but the Southern part and some of the Northern territory of Europe; in all, about one half the territory of the United States.

But now came the MODERN EUROPEAN civilization. Its area was at first Europe. The new nations of Italy, Spain, France, Germany, and England arose and stretched their influence farther and farther over the then known countries. The "Straits of Gibraltar" were no longer honored as the *termini mundi*—the ends of the world. The seats of ancient civilization were sought again. The new world of America was discovered, conquered, and colonized. The islands of the South Sea became known. The sea route to India was found, and expedition followed expedition, until at last the whole earth was known, and the ancient seats of glory, as well as the heretofore unknown and untrodden soils, were drawn into this general and cosmopolitan life of the human family. Civilization was no longer confined to the shores of the Midland sea, but it was girded by all the shores of all the seas. What were formerly the branches of the Midland sea became now the Atlantic and Pacific oceans, and those island kingdoms of former times became empires of whole continents. Such is Modern European civilization.

The last continent that joined this universal cycle, and the last race that took active part in this universal life, were AFRICA and the AFRICAN. The Northern shores of that continent, as we have seen, were but small belts of land, colonized by foreign races. The Arabs, even, knew comparatively but little of the great heart of Africa. It was left to the most modern missionaries of Selfishness and Civilization, of Trade and Religion, of Curiosity and Science, to open some insight into the life of the mainland. Untouched by the rise and fall of empires and civilizations, it had followed an isolated life. But unlike the Australians, the Africans had preserved a physical strength, which caused surprise to civilized man; and unlike the Indians of America, they had learned some agriculture and some industry, had some state life, and had reached some degree of culture, the most, even, in those parts which were least exposed to the inroads of the modern colonizer and trader. And this is the land—this is the race which was to furnish the modern slaves. While the Chinese were lingering along a half-civilized life, and the Hindoos were degenerating from their early culture; while Western Asia decked her soils with the broken ruins of former glory, and the Greek, even, grew in body and mind unworthy of their noble forefathers; while Western Europe, under the influence of the Germanic race, was rising to be the lawgiver of the world, and sent its colonists to all the distant lands on a mission of regeneration; while the Red Man of the New World was battled with until "he had to go toward the setting sun,"

Africa was destined to furnish the SLAVE of the day, the Slave of modern nations, the Slave *par excellence*, the Slave of the new, industrial, cosmopolitan, and Christian civilization!

This modern Negro Slavery is, therefore, indeed, a "peculiar institution." It arose not in times of barbarism, nor through accidental warfare of fighting tribes. It was, in this respect, *unique*, isolated, one by itself in time, place, and circumstances. When Slavery was everywhere passing away, this peculiar modern Negro Slavery first began. The slave was no longer the accidental captive in fierce battles, waged for glory, power, and fame, the delights of the ambitious barbarian. But in place of "glorious" wars, there came inglorious slave-hunts, for no other object than to make captives, to sell these captives as slaves to the civilized man of modern times, who was to take these slaves to distant lands and continents, to sell them again to others, where they, with all their descendants, are bound to labor and to toil during their lives. Slavery thus became *industrial*, like the whole world and its civilization, and lost all its romantic features of old. The continent last discovered was to serve as the principal theater for this Slavery, and the race last found was to be the Slave race.

The Spaniards introduced this Slavery very soon after the discovery of this Western World, whose virgin soil needed the labor of whole races. Hayti, the first free black land, was also the first slave land. Four months before the Mayflower arrived, slaves were already in Virginia, through the kind aid of Dutch sailors. Since that time, the merchants of the North and of the South, of the East and of the West, of this and of other lands and continents, have been zealously competing with each other in this once honored traffic in human flesh, and whatever stain and curse are connected with it rest alike on this whole land and on the whole modern world. White men soon accustomed themselves to own black men. The Spaniards, French, Dutch, English, Americans, all and everybody, owned Negroes, and sold and bought them, and used them as their slaves. Laws of discipline, and systems to regulate the relations of master and slave, soon engaged the statesmen of all nations, and filled volumes of their codes.

III.—NEGRO SLAVERY IN THE SOUTHERN STATES.

Though modern Negro Slavery has some peculiarities, it is still Slavery in all its cardinal points. Some may say that, in our days, a distinct race is set aside to be slaves; but this, even, can be found in other periods. The Greeks regarded the Scythian race as born for Slavery. Similar were the ideas of the old Germans in respect to the Sclavonians, and "barbarous" and "slave" were almost synonymous terms among the "civilized" nations of antiquity. These civilized nations, however, were sadly undeceived in after-times. If we thus would judge from the history of other kinds of Slavery to the future of our own, we should be forced to the conclusion that Negro Slavery, too, must have its growth, its modifications, and its end. The peculiar features which distinguish our Slavery from others, such as its mercenary origin, its industrial character, its growth in a period of great achievements in science and politics, which seemed to promise hope, and freedom, and happiness to the whole human race, these peculiar features would speak more in favor of modifications and a gradual abolition than in favor of a perpetual continuance. But why should we longer urge the argument of history? The whole question has already been decided in principle, and to a great extent in fact, too. For all civilized nations—whatever their other sore spots may be—and half of our States have emancipated the former Negro Slaves—the whole modern civilized world has long acknowledged that it is unjust and inhuman to receive, with chains and fetters in our hands, a new race, neglected and isolated. To reopen the slave-trade, and put again a degrading stamp upon *all* Africa, to doom the whole race and continent to be a perpetual and entire Slave race and Slave continent, none but a rash, thoughtless, and misguided politician can think or hope. The people of the whole civilized world stand ready with the weapons of the world to repel any further outrage on a shamefully treated continent. The question is, therefore, not whether *Africa* shall be a slave continent, and the African a slave *per se*, nor even that all the Negroes transported into our land shall be slaves forever, but the issue is only whether those NEGROES WHO ARE STILL OWNED AS SLAVES BY THE SOUTHERN STATES OF OUR UNION shall be slaves forever, or pass gradually into freedom, as it happened in ninety-nine other parts of the civilized world where Slavery had formerly existed. The question as to the continuance of Negro Slavery is, therefore, strictly an American—and, indeed, a Southern—question only.

Without solely relying, however, on our general argument, we will now shortly review the different special pleas which are here raised in favor of the continuance of Negro Slavery in the South.

IV.—THE PLEA OF THE CURSE.

God, or rather Noah, cursed the descendants of Ham, the father of Canaan. We read in Genesis ix. 25: " And he said: Cursed be Canaan; a servant of servants shall he be unto his brethren." There are a great many hermeneutical difficulties connected with this text. "Noah drank of wine and was drunken. * * * And Noah awoke from his wine, and knew what his younger son had done unto him." And then he cursed him. Now, this is quite natural; but it shows, as the venerable Thomas Scott says, " human imperfection in Noah" to drink wine; and especially, we may add, to drink too much of it, so as to get drunk. But, then—in all due reverence be it said—it would be quite natural, too, that Noah, awakening in or from his drunkenness, should use "imperfect" and intemperate language.

But, be this as it may, Ham showed a vile character in doing what he did, and he deserved strong punishment. Yet, why not only Ham, but also his young and thoughtless son, should be cursed, and not only he, but all the descendants of Ham—after the whole human race having been once most radically cursed in Adam—this remains a mystery.

Nor is it certain that God heard Noah's curse. To conclude *à posteriori*, from the misery and oppression of Africa, that God did hear this curse, such an argument we may object to in many ways. The African is by no means the most cursed of this earth. There is the history of the Aztecs, of the Australians, of the Fejeeans, and of many isolated tribes and races toward the North and South poles, with whom the African can fairly be compared to his advantage. With the exception of modern Negro Slavery, he has surely endured less misery than millions of Chinese and Pariahs. His numbers compare well with most of the half-civilized races, especially if quality is not overlooked. The men in the interior of Africa are intelligent, too, and mild, says LIVINGSTONE; and their peculiarly modern curse has been passing away this long time.

There are, too, some ethnological difficulties in this question. Some say the curse does not refer to the African Negroes at all. The Egyptians, the Phenicians, and the Carthaginians certainly were not of one and the same race with the Negroes. If Egypt is meant, there is certainly as much misery on the Nile as in the Soudan, or on the Mountains of the Moon.

But why should we endeavor to deduce our principles of social and physical action from the Book of the Soul-Life. The Good Book, we must repeat, has nothing to do with the outward forms of this life. And did it even curse the Negro, who among us Christians is ready to serve as the executor of this curse? But, especially we, the great Republicans and Free men of the modern world —shall we be the hangmen of Liberty? There is nowhere in the Good Book an express order given to us for that purpose, and there are but few who, on their own responsibility, would undertake the work on the ground of "drunken" NOAH's curse!

V.—THE PLEA OF RACE INFERIORITY.

There is, at least, no longer any dispute among the lovers of Southern Negro Slavery, whether the Negro is a man or a monkey; and the comparison of the Negro slaves to horses and alligators, or to *any* domestic or wild cattle, has become insipid, though it may come from the lips of clowns and punsters. The Negro is now generally regarded as a man, though an inferior man; and nobody will doubt that he is an inferior man if we compare him with the favored Caucasian of the present day. We will now examine somewhat the causes of this inferiority of races.

When we look attentively into the history of mankind, our eyes meet three great facts—we may call them Facts of Difference. There is first, at all periods, in all places, and at all stages of human culture, a Difference among Individuals, though they may belong to the same race, or nation, or family, even. It is a physical and moral difference as distinct as that of our faces. This is one of the great obstacles to those theories of communistic equality. No Spartan law of education, no Free-School system, no Forced education, no Democracy, no Religion, no Philanthropy has ever yet succeeded to make men equal, be it physically, morally, or socially.

This same difference appears when different individuals are connected and formed into associations, be they families, tribes, nations, or races. And this is the second fact. Just as the development of an individual depends upon his genetic structure, and upon the circumstances in which he is placed—or, in COMTE's language, upon the character of the organism and of the medium which surrounds it—so do, also, associations of any kind depend upon their inward genetic power and upon the outward influences. Among these outward influences are the geographical and physical condition of the respective lands, the degree of isolation from other tribes and nations, or of communication with them, the state of culture of these tribes at the time of contact, and the interest the more advanced societies take in lower and less advanced organisms. Should even the inward endowments of two tribes be the same, the difference of the circumstances that surround them might change their whole character.

The third fact is, that associations, like individuals, are born, grow, decay, and die at different periods and have different durations of life. This fact depends directly upon the second.

The workings of these three great facts have ever made the picture of the human world-life greatly variegated. Now nations arose, then they fell. One race was still lying in barbarism, while another was in the very zenith of its civilization. This same civilized race became weak and decrepit, while the barbarous one rose to strength and power. One people grew to the greatest perfection; another was arrested in the midst of its course. In the great history of the races and nations, we see, indeed, the same phenomena continually repeating themselves as in the history of the individuals of one and the same nation. But this is the necessary principle of all human development. Difference, indeed, is the element of all harmony. There have been, and there will ever be, different individuals in the same nation destined to fulfill different tasks and duties. Some will grow earlier, faster, and higher; others will ever remain in the lower walks of life. And exactly thus it is with the tribes, nations, and races of the whole human family. Different nations and different ages have different tasks to perform. Some will rise to magnificent dimensions, as their literature and art will bear witness in all generations to come. Such were the Greeks. Others will grow, too, but some grotesque temples and broken idols will be all that remains to speak of their former glory. Such were the old Mexicans. Some will remain barbarous during long periods, and be subjected and subdued at one time, but at length will gradually rise and set their feet upon the necks of their former victors. Such is the story of the Germans and the Romans. Some races will be interrupted in their long childhood; a more civilized race will fall upon them, and whatever germ there may have been in them, the more powerful race will destroy it. Such we learn from the history of the conquest of America and the "sinking away" of the Indians. Some will be entirely neglected and isolated, until they are so degenerate that they are forever lost, like the Australians. Others, again, have once had some civilization, but have sunk gradually to a lower level until they were aided by more advanced nations to rise again to higher life, though this be often a cruel process. Such is the story of the Hindoos and the English. There have been tribes, and even cultivated ones, of whom now the names even have passed away. Such are the Goths. There are others whose countries were decked with palaces of unheard-of luxury and splendor, which now are deserts and wastes for "wolves to howl in." Look to Asia for examples! Where are the proud Assyrians? The Northern temperate zone, the largest habitable land, must naturally remain the principal theater or the central part of all human culture. But has this favored zone ever saved from decay the tribes and nations that poured in upon it? No; the principle of degeneracy depends upon no clime or sun! It gnaws in the heart of the privileged Caucasian, who dwells near the center, as well as in the Patagonian's breast, who is hurled far off to the outer end of the radius.

Such has been, heretofore, the strange history of the world—a continuous up and down, and still a progress. And is history now to stop? Are there no more tribes, and nations, and races to come? Do not Asia, Northern Europe, and Africa yet harbor millions who seem to be waiting for their time to play some more conspicuous part in the world's history? Or, are we blind to the new comers who, from year to year, vindicate with greater emphasis their right to be among the nations?

In the face of these historical facts, what place can we ascribe to the African? He is among the latest comers. What prospect has he in this turmoil of human progress? The people of Africa seem certainly not lost beyond the hope of recovery. They do not look like a decrepit, wasted, and ruined race. Nobody can look at the muscular strength of the Negro, and call him the offspring of a dying race. Let us view him in Africa! They say he is inferior to us. Well; but is it impossible to raise him to any higher degree of culture? Who can affirm that, in the face of the most modern developments of our heroic travelers, VOGEL, BARTH, and LIVINGSTONE? There seems to be a difference in tribes among *them*, just as anywhere else. But, on the whole, they are not a people of the lowest character. Though they were isolated so many centuries, they did not remain mere hunters. They reached, by themselves, some agriculture, some manufacture, some commerce, some civilization. Or, if we view them in their contact with more civilized nations, they certainly are not void of the power of imitating. In Africa itself they have manufactures of iron slave-chains—the best that are made, they say. And here, our own experience does certainly not show that the Negro, North or

South, is incapable of progress. But how can we expect much from him in this our land? In the South he is a slave, all direct means of progress being withheld from him. In the North he was emancipated rashly, cast upon a world whose ways he did not know, generally unaccustomed to managing his own business or owning property; in a word, untaught in the lessons of liberty. Besides, he was thrown among a crowd of Yankees, Dutchmen, Irishmen, and Germans, all of them descendants of a race long civilzed, all eager after gain, and all skillful in obtaining it. How disadvantageous was the Negro's position here! How long, indeed, will and must it take him to rise to a level with us, who have the start of him by centuries of culture? Perhaps he will never reach us. But, that he is capable of some degree of civilization, who can deny, whether he may look upon the toils and feasts of the plantation, or upon the schools and huts of the North? And are there not many Negroes who have reached a higher intellectual standing in our community than ever can be reached by many of our own native or foreign population of Caucasian blood? No impartial man can look at the Negro here, and declare him incapable by nature of any progress. The Negro is a progressive being—a man, and not a brute.

But, suppose he can never reach the degree of the civilization of the Caucasian! Suppose he will ever remain as inferior to him as he now is! How can we arrive, from the fact of relative inferiority, at the necessity of Slavery? By what train of logic can we come to the conclusion that inferior races must be made slaves, and not only this—for Slavery may at first be best for them if we abstract from the manner of their coming here—but that they must be kept slaves *in perpetuum?* Must, then, *all* inferior races, and nations, and tribes be likewise made slaves? Well, then, we have plenty on our hands, and fillibustering will not cease until all Mexico, all China, all the Indies, all Patagonia, all Africa, all Asia, and a good part of Europe is enslaved! For such inferior tribes and nations are found everywhere—a little higher, a little lower. Where is the line beyond which there is no more freedom, but only eternal Slavery?

No, we Americans, a small portion of the civilized people of this world, and a portion of this small portion again, all lovers of liberty, we, the nation of the "happy and the free" above others, we can not oppose effectually the ways of the world, the voice of civilization, the lessons of History. The Negro *is* inferior, at least now; he may ever be so; but he is not therefore necessarily to be a slave, or, rather, the slave of the American cotton-field, forever, and with all his descendants!

VI.—THE PLEA OF PHILANTHROPY.

No man will ever plead philanthropy for the slave-trade. A heartless trader in human flesh presents himself, with an appropriate vessel, on the coast of Africa. There he meets a misled, barbarous chief. Excitement for gain prompts them both—the trader and the chief—to make a bargain. The trader lays down a heap of the good things of this world, which flatters the senses of the savage. The savage chief, in his turn, arranges a man-hunt, catches as many descendants of his race as he can get, and gives those who are alive and well to the trader in fulfillment of his bargain. The trader packs them, like so many beasts, into the infected hull of the slave-ship, carries them to a foreign land, and there again are sold as many as are alive after this second process. The man, who first was free, is then a slave, owned by another race, in another land, forever. Is that philanthropy? Is that love of mankind?

But let us abstract from the dark origin of Negro Slavery. Let us forget the millions who were transported before the foundation of our Free Republic and after it! Let us forget the demoralization which civilized man has thus thrown upon the newest comer among the races! Let us forget the demoralization which he has, to some degree, unconsciously loaded upon himself! Let us forget Humanity! Let us take Slavery as it is in our own Southern States! Suppose even the slave-ship, with all its horrors, is the messenger of philanthropy; suppose it was and is philanthropy to fetch the Negro from his native land, and make him a slave—is it philanthropy to keep him a slave after he has once quitted the ship, entered our land, unlearned his barbarism, taken upon himself the work of civilized man, and imitated his ways? Is it philanthropy to keep him down, or to destroy any little ray of progress that may indirectly strike the poor wretch? No, Philanthropy, above all, would teach us—after such great wrongs on our side and such favorable experiences on the other—to help the poor man, to give him the means of culture, to teach him the rudiments of civilized life, and to try, at least, like all nations heretofore, to make him an intelligent slave, whether this process may lead him to freedom or whether it may never break the chains of bondage. To treat him as a man, as an *anthropos*, Philanthropy certainly must demand of a man.

VII.—THE PLEA OF NECESSITY.

But who will work our cotton-fields? We now abstract from all philanthropy or humanity! Who will work under our burning sun? AGASSIZ says the white man can as well as the black man, or he may, we think, at least accustom himself to it. And LIVINGSTONE writes from Africa even: "I have never had a day of illness since my return. We find, too, that, so far from Europeans being unable to work in a hot climate, it is the want of work that kills them. The Portuguese all know that as long as they are moving about, they enjoy good health; but let them settle down and smoke all day, and drink brandy, then—not a word about brandy in the fever that follows—the blame is all put on the climate." The Germans, too, seem to get along, in every kind of thrift, very comfortably in Texas.

But suppose, even, that we need the Negro—and we, too, think we do—would we lose him by raising him to liberty? Not at all. If we teach him the ways of self-reliance and freedom, and treat him as other laborers, he will never leave what has become to him his native country. He will not come North, for he will prefer the warmer sun of the South, better adapted to his nature, and prefer the soil where he has learned to be free. He will prefer the work which he has learned to do, and the society which surrounded and aided him during his regeneration. For, that he can be grateful and is capable of patriotism the war of the Revolution bears ample testimony. Nor could he long to go back to Africa, which, indeed, has become to him a strange land. As little would he leave as the descendant of the European leaves his adopted fatherland to recross the ocean and settle in the old world, which now is as new to him as the Western world was to his ancestors. If the Negro were free, he would voluntarily stay here, where often force alone now keeps him. He would perform the lower duties of social life for generations to come, and in these lower walks he would remain, should he be incapable of ever competing with the old Caucasians. Surely, we want the Negro, and we shall have him, whether Free or Slave.

VIII.—THE PLEA OF SELF-INTEREST.

We find that everywhere in history where emancipation was gradually prepared and finally accomplished, the estates of the masters became many times more valuable than before. Examples are frequently given by the many writers on Slave and Free labor. The Count of BERNSTORFF is said to have lost one hundred thousand dollars by emancipation; but his annual income from his estates rose from three thousand to twenty-seven thousand dollars.

The Slave, as long as he works for his master, will generally be as lazy as the circumstances and the lash will permit. From this principle there arose those manifold computations of the economists and the various estimates of the comparative cost of Free and of Slave labor. But on the whole, they all agree that Slave labor is the more expensive of the two. And this is just what the South needs. Make the Negro more intelligent and skillful, and give him the hope of his future emancipation, then will his ambition soon tell upon the estates of the master. During this gradual process of emancipation, the master can only be the gainer.

TUCKER thinks that Nature seems to demand a certain ratio of the population of a country to its square miles before a master can emancipate his slaves with gain to himself. To apply the rule of an arithmetical means to a dozen examples of emancipation is rather venturesome. The principal and decisive condition of the master's preserving his self-interest in emancipation, is that it be gradual. In such a case it has never brought loss on any master in any example from history, whatever the above-mentioned ratio may have been.

IX.—THE PLEA OF THE CONSTITUTION.

We have here the last of the pleas generally heard in favor of the continuance of Negro Slavery in our Southern States. The plea of the Constitution! And, indeed, the Constitution alone can and does, in our eyes, recognize Slavery! But there it stands, that noble instrument, with the name "slave" carefully avoided. There stands at its side another cherished document—the Declaration of Independence—with its startling principle: "That all men are created equal; that they are endowed by their Creator with certain inalienable rights; and that among these are life, liberty, and the pursuit of happiness." Neither of these, our Primitive Laws, stamp the Negro to be a lower being than a man. This man may be your property, slaveholder! But—aside from any humanity—you still do not own him as you do "your horse or your ass." You know that you indirectly vote for him; you know that you can not kill him when he gets old, as you do "your horse or your ass!" You know that there is some little difference between owning him and owning "any other cattle!" You can not make him out a beast or a brute: not from the Constitution, not from any law of man, be it written or only secretly engraved in the human breast. You know that the Negro is a man! for this is, after all, the question. Man or Beast—this is the final issue! But our noble Constitution, in letter and spirit, abhors an interpretation which ambitious politicians would like to force upon it. Not "beast," or "brute," or "cattle," not even "slave," is the term given to the Negro! "Bound to service" is all that expresses the relation of slave and master.

Wherever provisions are made respecting slaves, they are so worded as not to stigmatize them as even a distinct caste or class. In Art. I., Sec. 2, persons "bound to service for a term of years" are classed with the free persons; and "all other persons"—meaning, in the language of the Constitution, "persons bound to service" without any qualification of time, or, in common language, slaves—are put on the same footing as the "Indians not taxed." Art. IV., Sec. 2, from which the Fugitive Slave Law is derived, is a provision against "persons held to service or labor in one State, under the laws thereof, escaping into another," and comprises obviously all persons, black or white, held to service for any period of time, however short or long. This provision includes slaves, but it is not made for them alone. The Constitution recognizes Slavery, to be sure, but not as a general, national, and hereditary institution, authorized by the laws of the United States as such, but as a local relation between master and slave, calling it expressly "service or labor in one State, under *the laws thereof.*"

But let us not with conscious willfulness misunderstand and distort the suggestions, hopes, wishes, and intentions of those "noble men who framed our Constitution and founded our Union," lest their desecrated memory pervert and crush us.

X.—REQUISITES FOR A TRULY PHILANTHROPIC EMANCIPATION.

Though our minds may now have given up all prejudices, and we may look with impartial eyes upon the fact of our Negro Slavery and its gradual emancipation as taught by history, still there are yet heavy obstacles in our way. May we be allowed to state what, in our opinion, are the primary requisites of a peaceful solution of this difficult question?

I.—DELICACY.

Negro Slavery exists only in some of our States. No earthly power can force it again on the Free States or on the world. Its local character is therefore a reality. But just on account of this local character of Slavery, the greater DELICACY is needed. If Negro Slavery still existed in all our States, and under similar circumstances, no party or section could be charged with ignorance of facts or intentional distortions and selfish interests. It would then be regarded as a common good, or as a common evil, or as a common necessity, and be discussed freely, like any other question, independent of locality. It would not rouse a whole section against another, and divide our country geographically as it does politically. It would be an easier work to get rid of a common enemy, and would need less care and delicacy in words and actions.

England was in a very different position from what we are. Slavery existed in one of her distant colonies or dependencies, which was but a small part of her empire. But *our* Slavery exists in our very midst; in sixteen co-equal States of our confederate republic. It is thus cherished in a considerable portion of our land, and it therefore needs great delicacy of treatment, unless we give up the idea of regarding ourselves as equal members of the same Union, and citizens of the same nation.

II.—POLITICAL NON-INTERFERENCE WITH THE SOUTH.

There is no doubt that the present Slave States once knew what a dubious guest they harbored in the Negro Slave. They had men as liberal, as wise, as noble, and as energetic as the men of the North, in whose words and teachings the policy best for their country was expressed, distinctly and unmistakably. Again and again did they publicly denounce Slavery, in language strong and decided: but the spirit of which could not be misinterpreted or suspected. They even contrived ways and means to gradually get rid of Slavery, and they had associations for that purpose.

The Southern States were fairly on their way toward a final abolition, just as the Northern. The latter were, however, their predecessors in this work from many other reasons than mere philanthropy. Climate, the character of their products, and immigration, made, from the very beginning, the negro slave less desirable and less necessary there than in the South. Still, the Southern States, too, thought of emancipation, though they were naturally to come last, and their work was to be slower, in the same degree that their peculiar geographical position, and their climate, soil, and production had allotted to them a larger number of slaves.

We will quote here some well-known passages from Southern writers, to see what the state of feeling on this subject was as late as 1832. Said the elder RITCHIE, in the Richmond *Enquirer:* "Means sure but gradual, systematic but discreet, ought to be adopted for reducing the mass of evil which is pressing upon the South, and will still more press upon her, the longer it is put off." He was referring to Negro Slavery. FAULKNER, too, said, at that time, in the Virginia House of Delegates: "Sir, I am gratified to perceive that no gentleman has yet risen in this Hall, the avowed advocate of Slavery. The day has gone by when such a voice could be listened to with patience, or even with forbearance." This was in 1832. Why did all these free words about "withering and blasting effects of Slavery" stop soon afterward? It can be proved with almost mathematical certainty what share the rash interference of Abolitionism had in delaying the work of the Free labor movement in the South. Let us here quote a memorable passage from DANIEL WEBSTER, whose clear-sightedness none will question. Referring to that same matter, he said:

"Let any gentleman who doubts of that recur to the debates in the Virginia House of Delegates, in 1832, and he will see with what freedom a proposition made by Mr. RANDOLPH for the gradual abolition of Slavery was discussed in that body. Every one spoke of Slavery as he thought ; very ignominious and disparaging names and epithets were applied to it. The debates in the House of Delegates on that occasion, I believe, were all published. They were read by every colored man who could read, and to those who could not read, those debates were read by others. At that time Virginia was not unwilling nor afraid to discuss this question, and to let that part of her population know as much of the discussion as they could learn. That was in 1832. As has been said by the honorable member from South Carolina, these Abolition societies commenced their course of action in 1835. It is said—I do not know how true it may be—that they sent incendiary publications into the Slave States ; at any event, they attempted to arouse, and did arouse, a very strong feeling ; in other words, they created great agitation in the North against Southern Slavery. Well, what was the result ? The bonds of the slaves were bound more firmly than before ; their rivets were more strongly fastened. Public opinion, which in Virginia had begun to be exhibited against Slavery, and was opening out for the discussion of the question, drew back and shut itself up in its castle. I wish to know whether anybody in Virginia can now talk as Mr. RANDOLPH, Governor McDOWELL, and others talked, openly, and sent their remarks to the press, in 1832? We all know the fact, and we all know the cause; and everything that this agitating people have done has been, not to enlarge, but to restrain, not to set free, but to bind faster the slave population of the South."

There can not be any doubt that Northern Abolitionism was one of the causes of the change of feeling in the South.

Abolition of Slavery can never be effected by a hostile political party in States in which there is no Slavery. For the South will never, can never, be *forced* into abolition. We abolished our Slavery in the North without any interference on the part of the South or the West, and the same privileges must be granted to the other States. Abolition of Slavery was heretofore effected by the action of separate States, and they consulted neither in regard to time nor manner with any other State. Each State acted by itself, and excluded all interference of others. They may have been influenced by the example of other States or nations, still they surely excluded all *political* interference either from the Federal Government or from single States. And such—State by State—will be the course of emancipation until the whole work is accomplished. The question of abolition ought, therefore, never to enter the mind of any Northern man as far as he is a member of a political party. In the abstract, everybody has a right to his opinion, but a political party is no agent for abstract schemes and wishes, but for such MEASURES as are best fitted for immediate political action. In belonging to a party, a man does not thereby become a traitor to his opinion; he only subscribes to the rationality and justice of certain political measures proposed. But abolition of Slavery can never appear as such a measure on the programme of any political party in the North.

Besides the impracticability of such an undertaking, it is against the Constitution, to which a political party, as a medium of political action, owes strict adherence. If we are dissatisfied with the Constitution, we ought not to cover our intention with false issues, but we ought openly to confess our plans, and employ all means prescribed for changes or amendments in that instrument.

Abolition of Slavery, as a political measure, belongs chiefly to the South. There are still, as in former times, fearless champions of freedom there to start the work again, and the initiative comes with better grace from their own men. The South will recover from its excitement. This very process of secession will be the means of opening its eyes again to the righteous claims of Freedom. There are now, in several Slave States, parties which dare to attack Slavery in some shape or other, and in some States their final object, abolition, is openly avowed. There, agitation is proper. It may have been silenced in these days of over-excitement. But this state can not last long. Times of prudence and peace will return, and the former work, though now interrupted, will be taken up again with renewed vigor.

Thus delicacy, reason, and the Constitution oppose alike all political interference of the North with the question of abolition in the South.

III.—PRUDENCE.

English emancipation, as we have above stated, can not serve as a model for us. But we have a warning example nearer at hand, in the abolition of Slavery in our own Northern States.

Though the lands, in the care of a numerous crowd of skillful and energetic colonists, did not suffer so much as in the West Indies, still the small minority of colored people found themselves in a condition very similar to that of the Negroes of the English colonies. Suddenly they passed from Slavery to a state in which they had to unlearn, or learn otherwise, what as slaves they had learned. They were like helpless children. They wandered around uncared for and homeless; they struggled with diseases, and lived, and still live, in poverty, being often in want of the necessaries of life. Liberty was, to many, a curse. It will take much more time, and cost many more sacrifices, before they are in a condition to profit by the advantages of freedom. Thence arose those facts which CALHOUN used in his Defense of North American Slavery, addressed to Lord ABERDEEN, though he mistook entirely the cause, for it is the MANNER of emancipation only which did the injury.

The only beneficial and satisfactory way of emancipation is the slow and gradual change and reform of the condition of the slave. We must instruct him in the elements of common and practical knowledge. This is the fundamental reform. Then we must, in the language of Mr. CAREY, accustom him "to possess and manage property"—reforms already partially introduced into some of our Slave States. The slave may be hired out by the master, as in some of our Southern cities. The field-slave may be allowed to cultivate, under the master's control, some acres of land for himself. As in Rome, the slave may be allowed to buy his liberty—reforms already applied to some extent.

Other aids in this slow work of emancipation might be suggested in different places; for true and beneficial emancipation can only be PARTIAL, LOCAL, INDIVIDUAL, and GRADUAL. We can not do it by one stroke! It is a complicated work, to which we all may lend our feeble hands. Some slaves would thus soon be made free; others would have to serve a longer apprenticeship for liberty. The Abolitionists and philanthropic men of all creeds and platforms may hasten on this work of love. They are liberal; let them, therefore, send their money to procure liberty for those who are deemed to deserve it. Let them then take care of them, and supply whatever the new-born freeman may afterward need. Let the Colonization Society, too, be aided in its work. Help to send to Africa those civilized Negroes who wish to aid their race in its progress! Let all who know new remedies and plans of peace be listened to, and all who can materially help, send their portions; while the slaveholding States themselves concert and advise and reform, until at last, this voluntary emancipation being nearly completed, State after State may seal, by a legal enactment, the *fact* of the Negro's freedom!

Should, then, any financial consideration delay the work of Humanity, or in any way thwart its purposes, there will be millions in the Union who will readily adopt *our* reading of WEBSTER's language when he says:

"There have been received into the treasury of the United States eighty millions of dollars, the proceeds of the sales of the public lands ceded by Virginia. If the residue should be sold at the same rate, the whole aggregate will exceed two hundred millions of dollars. If Virginia and the South see fit to adopt any proposition to relieve themselves from '*Slavery*,' they have my free consent that the government shall pay them any sum of money out of its proceeds which may be adequate to the purpose."

XI.—ACTUAL WORK ALREADY ACCOMPLISHED IN OUR OWN LAND.

On reading the wholesale denunciations which are so liberally thrown upon our republic, both by foreign and native writers and orators, it would, at first, seem as if our land and people had not yet done anything at all toward "gradual" abolition of Slavery.

Says G. F. KOLB, in his new work, "The Statistics of the World:" "There is no reason why we should accuse the American *republic* for the existence of Slavery; for Negro Slavery is a relic from the time when the land was under a *monarchical* government. But still, the guilt of not having limited that baneful institution, which is a disgrace to humanity, and of not having worked toward its gradual abolition, rests heavily on the modern republicans of America."

"Done nothing toward *gradual* abolition of Slavery!" We are accustomed to such language from the lips of high-souled theorizers, but we hardly expected to find it on the scientific pages of the "cool and calculating" statistician. Still, such seems to be the general language of the present day, to be mechanically repeated by each new self-appointed judge in the High Court of Universal Justice.

Has our national development really been so exceptional as to deserve the maledictions of the whole civilized world? Have we, indeed, not progressed at all toward greater freedom? Have we been steadily descending in the scale of civilization? Are we an anomaly in the history of modern nations? Or, can we show the same slow and gradual work of emancipation as they? We confess that our country might have done more if it had been more prudent and less selfish. But we have done *something*, and this something is worthy of the consideration of the world, before our final judgment is pronounced.

Let us look into our actual history!

I.—PROHIBITION OF THE SLAVE-TRADE.

The United States was the first nation to abolish the slave-trade. We take from the learned charge of Judge JAMES M. WAYNE the following data:

"The first act was passed on the 22d of March, 1794, when General Washington was President. It was intended to prevent any citizen or resident of the United States from equipping vessels within the United States, to carry on trade or traffic in slaves, *to any foreign country*. (Brig Triphenia *vs.* Harrison, W. C. C., 522.) That is, though slaves might be brought into the United States until the year 1808, in vessels fitted out in our ports for that purpose, they could not be carried by our citizens or residents in the United States in such vessels, *into any foreign country*.

"The next act of Congress was passed on the 2d March, 1807, when Mr. Jefferson was President. The act of 1807 begins by subjecting any vessel to forfeiture which shall be found in any river, bay, or harbor, or on the high seas, within the jurisdictional limits of the United States, or which may be hovering on the coast, having on board any negro, mulatto, or person of color, for the purpose of selling them as slaves, or with the intent to land them in any port or place within the United States.

"The act of 1818 prohibits the importation of negroes altogether into the United States, from any foreign kingdom, place, or country, without excluding the return to it of such slaves as might leave the United States as servants of their owners, comprehending such as have been employed as seamen on a foreign voyage.

"The act of 1819 authorizes the President, in a more particular manner than had been done before, to use the naval force for the prevention of the slave-trade, points out the circumstances and the localities in which seizures of vessels may be made, directs the distribution of the proceeds of them after condemnation, requires that negroes found on board of them shall be delivered to the marshal, what that officer's duty then is, and again commands that the officer making the seizure shall take into his custody every person found on board, being of the crew or officers of the vessels seized, and that they are to be turned over to the civil authority for prosecution.

"This brings us to the last act upon the subject, that of the 15th May, 1820. It denounces any citizen of the United States as a pirate, and that he shall suffer death, who shall become one of the crew or ship's company of any foreign [slave] ship; and that any *person whatever* becomes a pirate, and shall suffer death, who shall become one of the crew or ship's company of any vessel owned, in the whole or in part, or which shall be navigated for or in behalf of any citizen of the United States, or who shall land from such vessel on any foreign shore, and shall seize any negro or mulatto not held to service or labor by the laws of either of the States or Territories of the United States, with intent to make such negro or mulatto a slave, or who shall decoy, or forcibly bring or carry, or who shall receive on board of such ship, any negro or mulatto with intent to make them slaves.

"In the year 1823, the House of Representatives of Congress adopted a resolution to request the President to prosecute, from time to time, negotiations with the several maritime powers of Europe and of America, for the effectual abolition of the African slave-trade, and its ultimate denunciation as piracy under the laws of nations, by the consent of the civilized world.

"All the nations of Europe, as well as of America, have followed in the same legislation, and the object of the resolution of 1823 seems to be near its accomplishment.

"Upon three occasions since 1824, the subject has been under the consideration of Congress, and at each time has a determination been fully expressed to maintain the principles that have been incorporated into the legislation of the country.

There were several occasions, before and after these legal enactments, when the Congress of the United States expressed their abhorrence of the slave-trade. And this was and is a sentiment common to the great majority of people both North and South.

II.—ABOLITION OF SLAVERY.

At the beginning of our existence as an independent nation, in 1776, there were slaves in each of the thirteen original States.

TABLE XIX.—NUMBER OF SLAVES IN 1776.

[*Census Report of* 1850.]

States.	Number of Slaves.
Massachusetts	3,500
Rhode Island	4,373
Connecticut	6,000
New Hampshire	629
New York	15,000
New Jersey	7,600
Pennsylvania	10,000
Delaware	9,000
Maryland	80,000
Virginia	165,000
North Carolina	75,000
South Carolina	110,000
Georgia	16,000
Total	502,132

Other accounts give the number at 479,000.

Massachusetts, Rhode Island, New Hampshire, New York, New Jersey, Pennsylvania, all, at an early date, abolished Slavery within their jurisdiction.

Then, out of territory ceded to the United States by Virginia—the State which had at that time by far the greatest number of slaves, about one third of the total slave population of the Union,—we have formed the following States:

Kentucky	1792 (Slave)	Michigan	1837 (Free)
Ohio	1802 (Free)	And from Michigan—	
Indiana	1816 (")	Iowa	1846 (")
Illinois	1818 (")	Wisconsin	1848 (")

Thus, six of the thirteen original States have abolished Slavery within their territories, and six new Free States were formed from the territory of the Slave State of Virginia.

Vermont, too, was formed from New York in 1791, and Maine from Massachusetts in 1820. California, Minnesota, Oregon, and Kansas are new Free States.

To be sure, seven of the original thirteen States have not yet abolished Slavery, and nine new Slave States have been added.

But nobody can deny that we have done *something* "toward the gradual abolition of Slavery." For in 1776 we had nothing but Slave States, and now the majority of the States are Free.

Or, let us take the oldest and the newest Census of the United States, and compare the increase of the Free with that of the Slave.

Year.	Free.	Slaves.
1790	3,231,900	697,800
1850	19,987,500	3,204,300

The increase of the Free is thus 518 per cent., while that of the Slave is only 359 per cent. Freedom has thus increased at a greater ratio than Slavery, should we even take the above number unconditionally.

"But," says Mr. KOLB, "the proportion is reverse in the South; the slaveholders have succeeded there in bringing about an enormous increase of these unfortunates." To this we must decidedly object. The increase of the slave population is the greatest argument for the South. For it proves, on the whole, the good treatment of the slaves by their Southern masters. It shows, indeed—as we have had occasion to remark—the greater humanity of the Southerners when compared with other masters. But, however that may be, this can never be used as an argument *against* the South.

The work of emancipation, or gradual abolition, has

been steadily going on since the very beginning of our national existence. It commenced East and North, and gradually pressed farther toward the South and West. Nor did it halt at the boundaries of the present Slave States. It has already entered them, and is progressing there in spite of political and financial interruptions and disturbances.

III.—THE SPREADING O THE WHITE POPULATION

The present border Slave States are now the principal theater of action in this work of Freedom. We will first give a few tables showing the relation of the White to the Slave Population, and the increase of the former over the latter.

TABLE XX.—POPULATION OF THE BORDER STATES IN 1850.

[*From the United States Census.*]

States.	Whites.	Free Col'd.	Slaves.	Total Col'd.	Total Pop.
Delaware	71,100	18,000	2,200	20,200	91,500
Maryland	417,900	74,700	90,300	165,000	583,000
Virginia	894,800	54,300	472,500	526,800	1,421,600
Kentucky	761,413	10,000	210,900	220,900	982,400
Missouri	592,004	2,600	87,400	90,000	682,000
	2,737,217	159,600	863,300	1,022,900	3,260,500

TABLE XXI.—PROPORTION OF WHITE TO TOTAL POPULATION IN 1850. (IN PER CENTS.)

States.	1790.	1800.	1810.	1820.	1830.	1840.	1850.
Delaware	78.36	77.56	76.18	75.99	75.05	75.00	77.75
Maryland	65.26	63.34	61.78	63.88	65.12	67.70	71.68
Virginia	59.08	58.43	56.59	56.61	57.31	59.76	62.94
Kentucky	83.66	81.41	79.76	77.02	75.27	75.69	77.50
Missouri	—	—	82.64	84.08	81.73	84.41	86.79

TABLE XXII.—PROPORTION OF FREE COLORED TO TOTAL POPULATION. (IN PER CENTS.)

States.	1790.	1800.	1810.	1820.	1830.	1840.	1850.
Delaware	6.60	12.86	18.08	17.81	20.66	21.66	19.75
Maryland	2.51	5.73	8.92	9.75	11.84	13.21	12.82
Virginia	1.71	2.29	3.14	3.48	3.91	4.02	3.82
Kentucky	0.15	0.33	0.42	0.52	0.71	0.92	1.02
Missouri	—	—	2.91	0.56	0.41	0.41	0.38

TABLE XXIII.—MANUMITTED AND FUGITIVE SLAVES IN 1850.

BORDER STATES.

States.	Slaves.	Manumitted.	Fugitives.
Delaware	2,200	277	26
Maryland	90,300	493	279
Virginia	472,500	218	83
Kentucky	210,900	152	96
Missouri	87,000	50	60
	863,300	1,190	544

These four tables are intimately connected with each other.

The proportion of the White population had in 1850 risen, in per cent., in—

Delaware. Since 1820.	Maryland. Since 1810.	Virginia. Since 1810.	Kentucky. Since 1830.	Missouri. Since 1810.
1.74	9.90	6.45	2.23	4.15

The proportion of Free Colored persons had in 1850 risen, in per cent., in—

Delaware.	Maryland.	Virginia.	Kentucky.	Missouri.
13.15	10.31	2.11	0.87	2.53 (dec.)

Thus, the proportion of the White and Free Colored population was steadily increasing in the Border States; or, in other words, the Border Slave States are thus slowly and peacefully being transformed into Free States, and in some of them the work of Freedom is almost completed. The relative decrease of the proportion of the Free Colored population of Missouri is but a seeming exception. It was the effect of the extraordinary immigration of whites. Missouri rose in forty years, from the 22d to the 13th place among the States, Slave and Free.

The more extreme Southern States have as yet been less affected by the invigorating breath of Freedom which blows from the North. But, still, Tennessee seems to follow somewhat in the track of Kentucky, and North Carolina in that of Virginia, while Louisiana, by reason of its geographical position, its river, and its intimate connection with the Northwest, presents about the same features as the border Slave States.

POPULATION OF LOUISIANA IN 1850.

Whites.	Free Colored.	Slaves.	Total Colored.	Total Pop.
255,400	17,400	244,800	262,200	517,700

PROPORTION OF WHITE TO TOTAL POPULATION. (IN PER CENTS.)

1810.	1820.	1830.	1840.	1850.
44.82	47.83	41.46	44.96	49.35

PROPORTION FREE COLORED TO TOTAL POPULATION.

1810.	1820.	1830.	1840.	1850.
9.91	7.15	7.74	7.24	3.37

MAUMITTED AND FUGITIVE SLAVES.

Slaves.	Manumitted.	Fugitives.
244,800	159	90

Thus the proportion of the white population in Louisiana increased 7.89 per cent. The cause of the decrease in the proportion of the colored population is, as in the case of Missouri, due to the extraordinary immigration of whites. Missouri and Louisiana are the two Slave States which receive the greatest share of foreign and native immigrants. The five Border States and Louisiana together receive about 80 per cent. of the immigration to the whole South.

TABLE XXIV.—NATIVES OF THE FREE STATES AND IMMIGRANTS IN THE SLAVE STATES.—1850.

THE BORDER SLAVE STATES.

	Natives of Free States.	Foreign Immigrants.
Delaware	6,900	5,600
Maryland	23,800	51,300
Virginia	29,000	22,500
Kentucky	31,300	31,800
Missouri	55,600	76,200

THE WESTERN GULF STATES AND THE MISSISSIPPI.

Louisiana	14,567	67,200
Texas	9,900	7,400
Tennessee	6,500	5,300
Arkansas	7,900	1,300

THE CAROLINAS AND THE EASTERN GULF STATES.

	Natives of Free States.	Foreign Immigrants.
North Carolina	2,100	2,500
South Carolina	2,400	8,200
Georgia	4,200	6,500
Florida	1,700	2,600
Alabama	4,900	7,400
Mississippi	4,500	4,300

The flesh and spirit of the free white population of the North and of Europe seem thus to act as leaven in the work of emancipation in the Border States. The formation of a solid middle class of laborers, who neither are slaves nor keep slaves—the increase of the free colored population—the greater number of manumissions there than in other Slave States, in spite of the greater losses from fugitives—are facts intimately interwoven with each other. These States have thereby undergone such a change, and present such peculiar features, that it would be unfair to class them with the other Southern States. They are in a state of transition which makes them a class by themselves.

IV.—AMALGAMATION.

There is another force at work in the cause of Freedom. It is a physical force, but it acts as unconsciously as the social one we have just mentioned. It is the amalgamation of the white and the black races. The African and the Caucasian have never been connected so intimately as here. This country is in reality cosmopolite. Not only do the different branches of the same race—the Indo-Germanic—freely mingle with one another, but even two distinct races, in different stages of civilization, are here violently thrown into mutual embrace.

We will not now examine into the ethnological or the moral merits of such a mixture, but only state the influence it has on the social condition of the black race. And here one great fact stares us in the face, and that is: Amalgamation breeds freedom. It is as if the drop of blood from the ruling Caucasian, in the veins of the mongrel offspring, would never rest until the creature is as free as the creator. Let us see the general statistics referring to this matter!

There were, in 1775, about 479,000 slaves in this country. We were not able to find anywhere how many of them were Mulattoes. Still, according to the statistics of other years, they must have been proportionately but a small number.

Things have greatly changed since 1775. The Negroes must have freely mixed with the white population.

NUMBER OF BLACKS AND MULATTOES.

Year.	Blacks.	Mulattoes.	Total.
1775	—	—	479,100
1850	3,233,000	405,700	3,638,700

There were, thus, about as many Mulattoes in 1850 as there were slaves in 1775; and eleven per cent. of the colored population have a tincture of white blood.

NUMBER OF FREE BLACKS AND FREE MULATTOES.—1850.

	Total.	Slaves.	Free.
Blacks	3,233,000	2,957,600	275,400
Mulattoes	405,700	246,600	159,100

As, in the North, both Blacks and Mulattoes are free, we add a table of the Slave States only.

TABLE XXV.—NUMBER OF FREE BLACKS AND FREE MULATTOES IN THE SLAVE STATES.—1850.

THE BORDER STATES.

States.	Total Blacks.	Free Blacks.	Total Mulattoes.	F. Mulattoes.
Delaware	18,600	16,400	1,700	1,600
Maryland	143,800	61,100	21,500	13,600
Virginia	447,000	18,800	79,700	13,400
Kentucky	188,600	7,300	32,300	2,600
Missouri	75,800	1,600	14,100	931

THE CAROLINAS AND THE EASTERN GULF STATES.

States.	Total Blacks.	Free Blacks.	Total Mulattoes.	F. Mulattoes.
North Carolina.	281,900	10,200	34,000.	17 200
South Carolina.	377,000	4,500	16,800.	4 300
Georgia.	360,400	1,400	24,100.	1 500
Florida.	36,500	229	3,700.	703
Alabama.	321,800	567	23,300.	1 700
Mississippi.	290,400	295	20,300.	600

THE OTHER SLAVE STATES.

Louisiana.	228,300.	200	33,900	14,000
Texas.	50,600.	2,600	7,900	257
Tennessee.	221,700.	3,300	24,100	3,700
Arkansas.	40,900.	140	6,700	400

Still t is difficult to gı each State its proper share in this kind of Freedom's working, because there are no statistics respecting the emigration of Mulattoes to other States. We give, therefore, the general ratio only, which is sufficient for our present purpose. *Nine per cent. of the Blacks—but* SIXTY-FOUR *per cent. of the Mulattoes, are free.* It matters little how and through whose agency so many Mulattoes became free, though there is 1 Mulatto to every 234 white inhabitants of the North, while there is 1 to every 18 of the South; but 64 per cent. of the Mulattoes *are* free.

Thus amalgamation breeds freedom. There is no mistake in those simple figures. The black color, too, of the Negro bids fair gradually to pass away, and in some hundred years a genuine Negro will be a curiosity in this land of ours, especially a Negro slave. Still, as the Mulatto is more attractive than the Negro, amalgamation with the latter might stop. But nature has well provided in this regard. The Múlatto, as we have proved above, becomes free, and leaves his place to the Negro.

V.—COLONIZATION.

This is another agency in the cause of Freedom. The first American Colonization Society was organized January 1st, 1817—nine years after the abolition of the slave-trade. Since that time similar societies have been founded in many States. They all have the same purpose in view, and act with each other in harmonious concert. Some statistical tables will show how much has been done by colonization toward the " gradual abolition" of Slavery.

In order to get a little insight into the details of its working, we take the following table from the " Annual Report of the American Colonization Society," 1858.

FIRST VOYAGE, DECEMBER, 1856.

STATE.	Born free.	Slave.	By whom Emancipated.
Massachusetts	6	—	
Pennsylvania	1	—	
Maryland	1	—	
Virginia	—	11	Emancipated by will of T. Shearman, of Fauquier County.
Do	—	68	Emancipated by will of James H. Terrell, of Albemarle County.
Do	—	6	Purchased by the executors of J. H. Tyrrell.
Do	—	5	Given by their owners.
Do	—	4	Purchased their freedom.
Do	—	8	Emancipated by persons in Kentucky.
Do	—	1	Emancipated by S. R. Houston, of Union, Va.
North Carolina	—	12	Emancipated by will of Mrs. M. L. Gordon, of Hartford.
Do	—	1	Emancipated by Miss Charity Jones, Bladen County.
Georgia	—	1	Emancipated by Mrs. M. A. Williams, Savannah.
Do	—	1	Emancipated by will of J. B. Tafts, of Savannah.
Do	—	54	Emancipated by Richard Hoff, of Egbert County.
Alabama	—	3	Purchased their freedom.
Mississippi	—	1	Emancipated by C. C. West, of Woodville.
Kentucky	—	19	Emancipated by Harvey Berry, of Bath County.
Tennessee	—	4	Emancipated by will of Elizabeth Vanderson, of McMinnville.
Do	—	2	Emancipated by John Jipson, Sparta.
Do	—	7	Do. by Peter and Nancy Burum, of White County.
California	1	—	
Total	9	208	

From the same Report we made the following general table:

TABLE XXVI.—NUMBER OF EMIGRANTS SENT TO LIBERIA BY THE AMERICAN COLONIZATION SOCIETY AND ITS AUXILIARIES, FROM 1820 TO 1857, INCLUSIVE.

Year.	No.	Year.	No.	Year.	No.
1820	86	1833	270	1846	89
1821	33	1834	127	1847	51
1822	37	1835	146	1848	441
1823	65	1836	243	1849	422
1824	103	1837	138	1850	500
1825	66	1838	109	1851	675
1826	182	1839	47	1852	640
1827	222	1840	115	1853	783
1828	163	1841	85	1854	553
1829	205	1842	248	1855	207
1830	259	1843	85	1856	538
1831	83	1844	140	1857	370
1832	1,131	1845	187		

TABLE XXVII.—NUMBER OF EMIGRANTS SENT TO LIBERIA, FROM EACH STATE, FROM 1820 TO 1857, INCLUSIVE.

Massachusetts	34	Indiana	78
Rhode Island	36	Illinois	34
Connecticut	46	Missouri	83
New York	205	Michigan	1
New Jersey	35	Iowa	3
Pennsylvania	179	Texas	16
Delaware	5	Choctaw Nation	7
Maryland	543	Cherokee Nation	1
District of Columbia	104	California	1
Virginia	3,442		
North Carolina	1,283	Total number	9,872
South Carolina	415		
Georgia	1,030	Number born free	3,730
Alabama	105	Number purchased their freedom	332
Mississippi	536		
Louisiana	261	Number emancipated in view of emigrating to Liberia	5,810
Tennessee	697		
Kentucky	637		
Ohio	55		

The above does not include the number (about 1,000) that have been sent by the Maryland Colonization Society to the Colony of "Maryland in Liberia."

This is a work in which all States are co-operators, and all individuals may lend their assistance. It is wonderful what this American Colonization Society has accomplished with comparatively small means. It would only need greater liberality on the part of the United States, the States, and individuals to prosper the noble work still more, and make the little Republic of Liberia "one of the brightest hopes" of modern philanthropy.

The forty-third Annual Report of the American Colonization Society for 1860 refers to the "pressure of the monetary difficulties of the country," which the Society has felt considerably. But there is a little paragraph showing the effect of our political difficulties on the work of colonization, which we can not help giving in full:

"Emigration of Free colored persons has, from several causes, been retarded; but in the Northern and Middle States, during the last year, their thoughts have been directed to Africa, and they have sought knowledge of its advantages for their future home. *In the South*, this class, *in consequence of agitations on the Slavery question*, are exposed to new trials; in some cases compelled to leave the places of their residence, and we trust Divine Providence will direct their way to Liberia, where alone, at present, their highest interests can most certainly be secured and perpetuated. And surely common humanity (to say nothing of the spirit of the religion of Christ) demands, while these people are expelled from some districts of the South to seek in vain for comfortable homes at the North, that their friends should encourage and assist them to take possession of the great inheritance prepared for them by Providence in the land of their fathers."

CONCLUSION.

We have now passed over the whole ground of the social development of our question in all its principal phases, down to the present day. The general progress of humanity—the spirit of modern religion—the common origin of man descending from the same ancestral parents, and made after a common type—philanthropy, love of man in a narrower sense of the word, or love of everything created—the physical and the moral interests of the slaveholder—the spirit of the Constitution, and the incontrovertible "logic of facts" in our own history—all point toward protection and assistance of our brethren in bondage, toward a mitigation of their condition, and a gradual abolition. History has not spoken in vain for us, and Humanity is not an empty sound. We are no exception, no anomaly in modern progress. We have prohibited the slave-trade; we have directly abolished Slavery in some States; we have sent our missionaries of white flesh and free spirit all over our land; we have condescended to a generous amalgamation with the black man; we have civilized and colonized. These are certainly unmistakable symptoms of our passing, like other modern nations, onward toward greater freedom and GRADUAL ABOLITION.

Thus, everything points toward the gradual abolition of Slavery, and Slavery must and will vanish from our soil, except the infamous slave-trade be re-opened, or a new race be enslaved. But neither part of this alternative can be realized. We can not, in the face of almost unanimous resolutions in Congress, passed from the earliest beginning of our nation down to the present time, re-establish that world-desired traffic in human flesh. We can not so much despair in our present era as to believe that a gang of wily politicians might be found who would dare to undo, in a disgraceful moment, what a hundred noble years have done. No! no new slave will ever be imported by the consent of the United States, nor will ever a new slave be made, be he of African or other blood, through war or conquest. The time "for the repeal of the laws in the way of importation of bond-servants from Africa, and for the passage of proper laws to protect the same," will never come! That unsophisticated merchant who, from his retirement in Tivoli or Paphos, sent forth such words as the above to an "ignorant" North, will never be able to ship or see shipped a cargo of African flesh into the United States, nor will his children or children's children ever have that innocent pleasure.

But why is there now, in the face of all this irrefutable testimony of progressive history, so much struggling and battling on the part of some of us against this work of Freedom? Why is there such a violent stemming against Liberty, that most precious gift to man, so tenderly cherished by everything living? Is Freedom a curse, and Slavery bliss? Is Freedom weakness, and Slavery power?

And has not all this work been done *within* the Union? Why are there now cries and Ordinances of disunion and secession? What is the disturbing element which troubles the waters of peace and interrupts the work of Freedom?

But this will lead us to the *political* aspect of the question, which requires, indeed, our special and separate attention.

BOOK IV.

THE CRISIS.

BOOK IV.

THE CRISIS.

I.—THE BALANCE OF POWER.

THE new product of cotton, "which in 1794 was scarcely an item of export," gradually increased and made the slave more valuable to the South. This increase of cotton created a new interest, not known to the North, and even unimagined by the framers of the Constitution; and on it a new political machinery was founded; it was the so-called Balance of Power, into which all the Slave States were gradually drawn.

Whenever this force or interest appears in one and the same nation, the term "Union" has almost lost its power, and "Harmony" alone can take its place. Balance of Power is the sign of the existence of a "diremptive" or centrifugal force somewhere. Common attraction has ceased, and Balance of Power is only the artificial glue to keep together heterogeneous elements. But this struggle for Balance of Power became a definite historical fact in the same measure that the geographical sections became more distinct and separated. The South required now for every new Free State a new Slave State, and the old Constitution was "squeezed," and bent, and interpreted to suit the new wants. The noble founders of our Union, and the framers of our Constitution, did not foresee such a state of things. They did not suspect the so speedy arrival of King Cotton and Queen Balance with their respective suites. But these royal guests have arrived! They have been here a long time, managing and developing their forces! They are of a grasping stock, too! They have a Manifest Destiny to help them along. They hold a brilliant court, and their followers and armies are well fed and well rewarded with offices and honors! They have the Spread-Eagle for their colors, though, in their enlarged patriotism, they never forget themselves entirely. They have procured Texas "for the Union." They have obliterated that awkward line drawn across "a common country." They have endeavored to carry their ideas into all the new States and Territories. They are liberal enough to carry their "property" there, too, in all its different shapes, and work it for the more rapid progress of those new lands. They see, themselves, the wrong of Balance of Power in a Union, and therefore do their best to make this vast empire one, united, and common in everything; in hearts, in hands, and in all sorts of property, landed and personal, immovable and movable, black and white. That they are earnest in their purposes, they have lately shown in Kansas, though they may have, at times, met with failures. That they have pluck and do things thoroughly, they have most recently proved by hanging all they could procure, or keep alive, of the Harper's Ferry men. But, *these are not things that grow over-night, or reach to such dimensions by inward strength only.* They needed the care of outsiders, and they had it, indeed, most effectually. The North, with hot-house tenderness, kindly kept off all the cold blasts, and thus aided the growth of the Political Power of the South. "The North, for some reason," says DANIEL WEBSTER, " never exercised their majority efficiently five times in the history of the government, when a division or trial of strength arose." Among the courtiers around the new-born throne, we saw, therefore, representatives of all the States of the Union, South and North, East and West, and the royal couple never rejected outlandish applicants. It gave the court a more cosmopolitan air when all the climates of this Western World, those where the "colored people" dwell, and those where the "Niggers" grow, sent their pale sons to join in doing homage.

But the whole court has for some time been growing old and feeble. Its usurpation in obliterating the political compromise line of Freedom and Slavery was the culminating point of its power. It violated the humble *Magna Charta* of Freedom, and then commenced the days of trouble and dissension, as was prophesied even by Southern Statesmen.

The feeling of indignation soon gave itself vent in bitter words. The halls of our legislatures resounded with the most passionate language. At last it came to bloody acts. The most cowardly assaults were hailed as deeds of valor. Threats of disunion were soon everywhere uttered, as indifferently as if there was no such word as Treason in the laws of our land. Northerners were driven from the South, and Southern youths were eager to flee from the "pestilential air of Northern Abolitionism." The frontiers of the two sections were strewn with the bones of murdered citizens, slain by brother-hand. The gallows of JOHN BROWN was gloomily towering over the once sacred Mason and Dixon's line; and now, shooting, lynching, and hanging are the regular order of the day. But Kansas is free, and the party raised on account of Southern usurpation has at last gained the victory.

"One evil never comes alone." King Cotton lost, at the same time, his monarchical privileges all over the world. There are now many lands rising which dare to compete with his universal power. Thus, disappointed in his hopes and thwarted in his plans, King Cotton lost his temper, began a family quarrel, dismissed his cherished old queen, Lady Balance, and allied himself to Dame Secession, young and sprightly in appearance, but treacherous and rotten at the core. In anger he leaves his old mother Union, builds a new home, a new capital, and a new throne, where he can, undisturbed by the groans of Freedom, feast alone and forsaken on the hallelujahs of Slavery.

In order to reach his object and satisfy his ruling tendency, he is ready to nullify, to secede, to separate, to break the Union; to fight, and slay, and be slain—all for the sake of Power and Rule. He wants to draw into his modern hexarchy all cis-Masonic States, from which even the Albino courtiers of the North shall henceforth be excluded.

But let us dismiss all personifications and figures, and face the present trouble in all its gravity.

The American question has gradually become one of nationality. The establishment of the Missouri line, drawn through the midst of a common country, was one of the first great political onslaughts against our nationality. It was, indeed, the first step toward denationalization. Under the protection of that line, that unnatural element of Balance of Power grew until it was forced to turn either into Supremacy or Secession. Thwarted in the former, the South had only the latter to rely upon. Had it not been for that political interference, the American question would never have assumed the present character.

II.—SECESSION.

Since the Constitution of the United States contains no special provision for the case of a State wishing to secede from the Union, the inference might be fair that States have no constitutional right of secession. The Constitution seems even positively to prohibit secession. We read in Art. II., Sec. 10: "No State shall, without the consent of Congress, lay any duty of tonnage, *keep troops*, or ships of war, in time of peace, *enter into any agreement or compact with another State*, or with a foreign power." Even the preparatory steps necessary for secession seem thus to be forbidden by the Constitution. But should the South seek to evade the letter of the Constitution by a *separate* secession, it would undoubtedly violate its spirit. MADISON's words: "The Constitution requires an adoption *in toto* and forever!" are generally acknowledged to be the fair interpretation of that instrument.

But we will leave the question of the constitutionality of secession undecided. We will even suppose that the Constitution does not prohibit secession. In such a case we must have recourse to general political reasoning and to arguments from history. We will take the popular view of "State," for otherwise the question would be decided in a moment.

If this Union is a mere compact for an indefinite number of years, its end, as its beginning, must depend upon some act of mutual agreement between the parties concerned.

In making the original compact, certain conditions were entered into by the parties, and certain duties were imposed upon them, expressly or by the very nature of the compact. Should even all these duties and conditions have been complied with on the side of the party wishing to secede, an unceremonious withdrawal would be illegal and cause a total forfeiture of all claims on the common property. In any case, then, a consultation with the different members of the compact seems to be necessary, previously to a positive act of open secession.

Such cases are nothing novel in the history of states, and they were long since formalized by writers on Public Law. GROTIUS, thus, agreeably to the above reasoning, sums up the whole matter by saying: "A state which had been one, may be divided, either *consensu mutuo*, or *vi bellica*." "Mutual Consent" or "Force of War" is thus the alternative given by the "Father of the Law of Nations," the first authority in Public Law, even to the present day. "Mutual Consent" is, however, the first clause of that alternative, and "Force of War" is consequent only upon a failure of the first.

Almost all cases of a similar nature in modern history verify the above alternative and the order of its succession. The way by "Mutual Consent" was first tried, and only when all peaceable means were found futile, was "Force of War" resorted to.

Such is the history of the Netherlanders, of world-wide fame. For many years they had endured the blighting breath of the Spanish tyrant. They had felt each new wrong, each new insult, each new disgrace thrown upon them by a fiendish power. They protested, they petitioned, they prayed for justice, they remonstrated, they sent delegates to the King, they opened negotiations, they sued for redress; and only when petitions and remonstrances, conventions and negotiations, brought about no definite result, they raised their arms to fight for their rights, they seceded and declared their independence of an unfriendly government.

Such, too, was the history of our own United States two hundred years later. We were similarly circumstanced and acted similarly. We, too, petitioned and protested, convened and negotiated, and only when remonstrances and threats proved futile, was war declared and independence achieved.

These are the two most brilliant examples of secession in modern history. There are others, memorable, too, but less successful. Poland could not recover its independence. Hungary was ruthlessly delivered to Austria. In others still, secession was less bloody, as in the separation of Belgium from Holland; and Neufchatel, the Swiss canton, went, indeed, quite peaceably out of the guardianship of Prussia.

But there is an example of secessionary character in a country which bears great resemblance to our own. It is in Switzerland, a republican confederacy like ours, only growing less slowly into a united nationality. In 1846, several cantons or states resolved upon setting up a "Sonder-bund," a separate league. But the federal authorities, backed by the patriotic masses of the other cantons, tarried not long in deciding which policy to choose— that of coercion or that of "*laissez faire.*" A federal army was sent against the rebels, and in spite of Austrian arms and Catholic money, the secessionists were conquered, and Jesuitism, the bone of contest in that case, was hurled from the territory of united Switzerland. What Jesuitism was there, Slavery is here. We will examine whether such a "Jacksonian" policy would suit the present circumstances.

III.—OUR POLICY.

Which policy will now be expected on one side and on the other? What will the South do, and what the United States?

These Southern States which are eager after revolutionary fame, might undoubtedly profit by the two great models we cited. We can not expect so much humility as in the early days of the Netherland struggles, nor so much patience as in our own American revolution. But the chivalric Southerners ought not to be behind the sturdy Dutchmen, or the valiant Americans of old, in the ways of gallantry and manliness. They ought, certainly, to show as much frankness and forbearance toward a free republic as those early heroes showed toward despotic kings. They ought first to endeavor to obtain retrievance for their injuries, real or imaginary; and even in the case of a temporary refusal of their requests, they ought, as freemen and republicans of the nineteenth century, try again all peaceable means to avoid a violent disrupture of the once cherished empire. It can only be lamented that some of the Southern States have taken a different course, a course unwise and fatal to their best interests.

And what might we reasonably expect from the central power of the United States, from the Union as such? She would listen to the grievances which are given as cause for secession; she would endeavor to remove this cause, should those grievances be found to rest on real injustice done to the respective parties by the republic; she would construe and interpret the Constitution, the principal and fundamental bond of our Union, in the liberal spirit of this enlightened age; and should those grievances be found to be mere fancies, she would try to convince the rebellious States of their unjust and injurious policy; and, lastly, if negotiations and persuasions should be of no avail, she would be tempted, from love of peace, rather to let a State go than to incur the responsibility of the horrors of a civil war.

And still such a yielding policy would awaken some fear for the future of the empire even in the most peace-loving breast. Where and when would secession then stop? If the "sovereign" States have a right to secede, what would hinder us from breaking into thirty-four separate and independent republics? Further still, *we*, the "sovereign" people of these United States, have established this Constitution! Would not the "sovereigns" of each State, then, have the same right of breaking it as the States, or even more than they? What would hinder the city of New York from seceding? What, other cities, and counties, and islands, and townships? Whither would this "separatism," "this disorganizing individualism," lead us? "Would not," in the words of TAYLER LEWIS, "a political death come over what before was full of social life, and society be decomposed in its individual elements, and no longer be a BODY, but a *Mass*—a mass of putrescent and fermenting atoms?"

We are not yet near such a stage of perfect disorganization. But it is clear that a yielding policy would not save us from that danger.

This consideration will be weighed in the minds of patriotic statesmen North and South, and will influence their action.

It would have been much easier to secede in the earliest days of the republic and of the new Constitution. There were, at that time, thirteen little colonies scattered over a large surface. Each little colony formed a province or State by itself. Each had a small population, and was often separated from the others by large wastes and impassable woods, or alienating prejudices. A single glance into the history of those thirteen different settlements, a mere look at a geographical map of that time, must disclose the secret. They were as yet but loosely connected, and their principal bond of Union was at first merely a common opposition to a common enemy.

But what a different aspect the country has now, after a united growth of nearly a century! The frontiers between the different States are obliterated. The enlightened population increased and spread over woods and wastes. The once separated States blended and grew into each other, and had we now to form a new Confederacy, a new Constitution, a new State, a new Nation, would it ever enter our minds now to make a dividing line between Connecticut and Rhode Island, between New Hampshire and Massachusetts, between Delaware and Pennsylvania and Maryland? What need would there be of such a number of Governors and Capitals and separate Legislatures and other political machinery in the New England States? And we might multiply our examples. But it is sufficient for the present purpose to point out the undeniable fact that we have all, land and people, grown more and more into a better, united, and more compact body, whose period of epiphysis is almost over, and has thus caused such an intimate connection that any separation of its members would leave an open, if not a fatal wound. Several Southern States, carried away by the first excitement, and aided by a wavering policy of the federal government, may make secession a *fait accompli* on paper. It seems highly probable that this will be the face the matter will take. But this very non-opposition will allay the passion of the seceders, and they will soon awake to a consciousness of the fearful position in which they have placed themselves; for the PEOPLE can not, for any long period of time, remain blind to the immeasurable advantages of a common Union, and the unavoidable injuries and calamities arising from Disunion.

This growing together, this united national life, is even the very distinguishing characteristic of our present wonderful civilization. Germany is panting for unity, and has made the preparatory steps for its accomplishment. Italy has inaugurated a more poetical and radical method of reaching the same end. The republics of Central America are laboring under the same process, and South America appreciates slowly the merits of union.

History clearly shows that Disunion of parts that properly belong together, is fatal in the end. There is Holland, formerly so powerful, and Belgium, and the Hanse towns, and the Italian republics. "Individuals," says the famous FR. LIST, "owe the greatest part of their productive power to the political organization and to the power of the country in which they reside. A considerable population, and a vast territory, with varied resources, are essential elements of normal nationality, fundamental conditions of moral culture, as well as of material development of political power."

There is among a united people less fear and insecurity,

and, consequently, less waste of labor; a more steady industry, and a more reliable market. The policy of even friendly foreign states changes often unawares, and causes disappointment and loss beyond their own limits. There are no fortresses needed to protect the many boundaries, no troops or vessels to watch possible encroachments, no turnpikes or custom-houses to guard against foreign competition. There is free communication, free commerce, free trade, in the largest and most essential acceptation of the word; unfettered exchange of products, unfettered intercourse of men. This is the free trade for which the greatest statesmen and economists were laboring through so many centuries against that self-splitting system of feudal seclusiveness and dismemberment. Those heroes are now ignorantly thrown in the category of the narrow-minded modern free-traders, who, in their eagerness after foreign trade, forget the labor, freedom, and consolidation of their own country. Free trade is, indeed, a vital principle of a nation's life, if it means free commerce of men and produce, not on principles of privileges inherited or newly granted, but on principles of the equal interests of all individual members and states, of common sympathy, of a common policy, and a common destiny. Free trade in this sense creates fresh stimulus, new thrift and enjoyment, security and reliance, peace and power, an accumulated and multiplied force, and leads a nation, as a compact body, toward one common object.

This is what is meant by Union; this is what is meant by Nationality; and these advantages are either already at our command, or they are growing upon us so much the more exuberantly as we diligently watch our Union, ward off its dangers, reform its abuses, regulate its government, and understand our mission. We have, indeed, already become one of the Great Powers of the world, with the duties and privileges incumbent upon such a glorious rank. We, the people, have labored together this long time for a common destiny, in spite of political disturbances. The world has learned to know American industry, American commerce, American art, American civilization. We have perceived more clearly from day to day that we have a common destiny, a common mission to ourselves, to America, and to the world. And such a united growth has, in spite of the invectives and misrepresentations of political parties, laid the foundation for a solid Love of the Union, which needs but a moment of unbiased self-consciousness to rouse it to unheard-of deeds of patriotic valor.

Now, such thoughts will bear upon the minds of the people in all parts of our common land, and forebode a better future. But, in view of these undeniable facts, the country will also wake up to a true sense of its responsibilities. For we may, in the end, reach our common object, pointed out to us by Nature; but wavering counsels and lack of decision may make us pass through years of unnecessary suffering and misfortune. It is the best policy to face at once the whole danger. There is more at stake than the welfare of the Negro Slave. A nationality, a republic, a Great Power of the world, American civilization, the progress of the whole world, are in question, and the United States can not allow herself to be split or give up any part of her territory which is positively necessary for the accomplishment of her fundamental plan and the realization of the original idea which called her into being.

IV.—INTEGRITY OF THE UNION.

There are certain parts of a nation's territory which are positively necessary for the nation's existence. These may be called its *integral* parts. Other districts, provinces, or states may be less necessary, and the nation's destiny may be reached without them. Now, no *integral* part can be allowed to secede if the nation is true to itself, to its original plan, and to its mission. No failure, be it from lack of patriotism or from downright treason, can ever alter this political axiom.

The only question will, then, be : What are to be regarded as integral parts of the United States ? Under this name we must first comprise all *national* property—viz., property held by the United States for the purpose of protecting and defending itself against any encroachments, political or commercial. Such are all national "forts, magazines, arsenals, dock-yards, and other needful buildings," thus specified in the Constitution. They are necessary for two purposes—namely, for repelling the attacks of a hostile power, and for collecting the revenue. And they will remain to be necessary, whatever the policy of the United States may be during the long internal process of secession. We say "long," because actual and total secession is not the work of an Ordinance ; it would take a State months, and probably years, to break entirely loose from the Union and reconstruct a separate and independent government.

Especially must those forts and buildings and magazines be kept (during that whole process) which *protect the United States boundaries.* For if certain States should even be allowed to secede, and should actually secede, the

United States would, by such separation, receive a new boundary line, and this boundary line would be entirely exposed. In case of war, she would be entirely unguarded on that whole line, and be open there to any surprise; and even in peace she could not protect her commercial policy against smuggling and other foreign encroachments. There could thus, even in case of a yielding policy, not be the faintest doubt about the right and duty and present policy of the United States in regard to her national property. She would be obliged to keep her old forts and posts of revenue, whatever her final policy in regard to secession might be, until a new *cordon* of fortifications and customhouses could be established along the new boundary, and all other national works, made necessary by a separation of States, could be completed. She must keep them, defend them, and in case of treason or defeat, retake them. Anything short of this would be cowardice and treason, and would bring the curses of the nation and of the world on the head of the Executive.

Let us now examine the character of the STATES themselves that think of secession, or have passed secession ordinances. We begin with TEXAS.

Without entering into the political history of that State, it will need no argument to prove that its annexation was entirely unnecessary for the preservation, or growth, or position, or power of the United States. Its conquest may have been a necessity by reason of Balance of Power, but neither its climate nor its soil, neither its geographical position nor its people, made its annexation a necessity for the Union as such. To be sure, it cost us heavy sacrifices of blood and money. But Texas would not be worth a civil war, for the Union can and would stand without it. Texas may, therefore, be allowed to "slide off" South, East, or West, and become an independent State or a joint member of others.

We must, once for all, dismiss the common popular belief that we can prosper only by spreading over a larger area. We have enough territory, or rather more than is needed for centuries to come. We have no superfluous force to send off into foreign states or lands. We have plenty to do in what is already ours. There is yet an immense amount of our own land to be settled, cultivated, and watched over. We have not now, nor had we ever need of any part of Mexico, foreign to us in everything. We have no force to spare for its colonization. What we did in that regard, we did at the cost of our own peace and prosperity, without any benefit to us. As a Nation, we have no need of Mexico. As a Great Power of the world, the duty of guarding her does not devolve upon us alone. An American policy, strictly American, with the United States as Supreme Judge over all matters concerning the continent of America, is an anachronism and an absurdity. The world is no longer disconnected or inaccessible in its different parts. There are Great Powers of the world to whose *surveillance* no quarter of the globe is a stranger. And *they have as much right here as anywhere else, and we have as much right anywhere else as here*, or would have, if our narrow foreign policy allowed us to see our true position in the world.*

To CALIFORNIA the same reasoning would apply as to

---

* This will be the subject of a work by the author, now in course of preparation. Title: "The Five Great Powers of Europe and the United States of America."

Texas, were it not for its gold. But this exception is, after all, but imaginary. We needed California just as little as we needed Texas. The same amount of labor and capital invested in any one of our older States or Territories would have done much more to increase the wealth and to consolidate the power of the United States. We were spreading over our older lands with a speed greater than was beneficial to us individually or as a nation, and terrible were, and are still, the sufferings of those thrown to the outskirts of the inhabited and civilized part of our empire. They pass through years of misery and famine before they attain the most necessary comforts of a civilized life. Imaginary cities and paper railroads allure the weary laborer, eager to obtain a free homestead. The commercial policy of the nation and political speculations conspire with each other to send new crowds of emigrants to the West. And, indeed, the sparse lands of the first pioneers could be aided in no other way than by sending out new men and new money: otherwise they would have perished. The only difficulty was, and is yet, that, though Europe sends annually hundreds and hundreds of thousands to aid the spreading of cultivation and the extending of our area of active power, still the flood is too feeble, the number of immigrants too small; for speculation is ever paving a new West, whose end seems never to be reached.

While, then, this process of wasting dispersion was going on in the older part of our empire, a dispersion which only the superhuman exertion of the emigrants from the East and from Europe could keep from becoming an entire dissolution, California, on the extremest point of our national surface, was, with golden cords, violently drawn into the same system of diverging. Still more distant, and less connected with the older part of the nation, it required new waste of labor and capital to keep up a commercial and political connection. It once retarded a financial crisis, but it could not prevent it. We imported from Europe, at a fabulous rate, the fabrics of foreign labor; we paid with the agricultural products of the South and of the West; we spread over new lands to wrest from our virgin soil new products for foreign exports; we sent stocks of every description and name, public and private, to our creditors beyond the ocean; but all our exertions to keep up some show of balance were in vain; we needed the costly erection of a far-off workshop in the mines of California, to delay the final crash. The chance of gaining wealth with little labor, to be sure, gave an extraordinary impulse to human adventure; and life, labor, and capital were recklessly thrown away to feed the Golden Calf. But, had we kept our hands and capital at home, had we built up our own industry, melted our own iron ore, and fabricated our cloth, we would now be less dependent upon our own and foreign merchant princes; we would be richer, and stronger, and happier, and more civilized, though we had never known of the gold mountains of California. Gold is a product like others. It can not be obtained without labor. Labor is the measure of its value as it is the measure of the value of any other product. Nor is it a more necessary article of wealth than cloth or iron. There is no need of gold as a circulating medium. The world could at least have done without California or Australia. Then, as an article of manufacture, it is a luxury, and has its substitutes.

Still we *have* California, and we must do our duty toward her. The Pacific coast would naturally have been the last of all the lands of the United States to be drawn into a common national life. The commerce with Asia would scarcely have necessitated an exceptional course. A Pacific Railroad, to have benefited at once the whole empire, must have led through a chain of settled lands. But the extraordinary history of California requires extraordinary measures, and therefore the Road is a national necessity. However, should California wish to secede, the nation would save new expenses, and probably new struggles, and soon recover from a *momentary* disturbance of its commercial and industrial life. But the Gold State knows its advantages too well to desire secession.

Our relations with LOUISIANA are far different. The whole old territory of Louisiana was bought from France. It was bought by the United States, not by one particular State, or for one State, but by the whole and for the whole—for a common national purpose. It was bought, not for its people alone, but especially for its land and its river. In the earliest days of our republic, the Mississippi, down to its very mouth, was considered as *necessary* for the development of our Western Territories. The Western people, even in those early times, saw plainly that they could not do without a *permanent* and *undisturbed* right of freely navigating the Mississippi. Such a right, however, could be "undisturbed and permanent" only when the whole river was in their possession. They knew this; it was a general Western thought—nay, more, a common national thought, shared by all people and all statesmen. The Western people, therefore, laid plans for seizing New Orleans, even while it was yet Spanish. No wonder, indeed, that Jefferson used such decided language about its acquisition, and that Bonaparte, from whom it was at last purchased, said: "This accession of territory strengthens forever the power of the United States."

The Mississippi Valley, drained by the Mississippi and its tributaries, contains an area of over a million square miles. It is nearly as large as the slopes of the Pacific and the Atlantic together, and one third larger than the whole domain of the republic upon the adoption of the present Constitution. (Census, 1850.) In future centuries it may be a great republic by itself—the Great Republic of the Valley of the Mississippi, a friendly sister of a Great Pacific and of a Great Atlantic Republic. But at present, and probably for some centuries to come, such a separation will not be necessitated by any demands of self-interest, of executive expediency, or of economy.

Now, the mouth of the Mississippi is to the West, and thus to the United States, the same as the mouth of the Thames is to England, or that of the Rhone to France, or that of the Volga to Russia, and it will be claimed as a national river, and be defended as such.

Therefore, we must expect many and earnest efforts on the part of the United States to keep the extensive territory of old Louisiana and the present State in harmonious connection with the main body. It is, beyond the faintest doubt, an *integral* part of the Union, and will regard itself as such, and be so regarded. Patriotic counsels and common interests will tend to suppress undue excitement and re-establish peace and harmony.

We now come to the BORDER SLAVE STATES. Looking at their position between the number-filled North and the more thinly-settled South, we might conclude *à priori* that their greatest attraction lies Northward. The force of attraction is in proportion to the force of production, and this again is so much the greater as the population is the larger.

This theory is proved by practice. The principal exchanges of the Border States are with the States north of them. Moreover, the chief product of their Southern neighbors is not carried to them directly. It is taken to the far-off seaports, and then it is shipped to Europe, and thence again to their Northern neighbors, until at last, after a long and costly circumambulation, it arrives at their homes from the side exactly opposite the one from which it started. (And this is probably the way which cotton is to go for a long period of years, whether there be secession or not.) Thus this very Southern staple rivets still closer the Border States to their Northern friends.

Their population, too, and their whole progress show, in spite of Slavery, unmistakable signs of sympathy with the North. (See Tables on page 118.)

Under the ægis of a common nationality, the white population gradually pressed down into the Border Slave States, which were thus—we repeat—slowly and peaceably being transformed into Free States. Had it not been for political disturbances, this process would have gone on still more rapidly. It is the way prescribed by nature for freeing States, and the work is done unconsciously on the part of the immigrants from Europe and the North, but it is none the less surely done. There was thus a living and lasting tie forming between the Border Slave States and the Free North, and all boundary lines were vanishing.

And this was undoubtedly the cause of the steady increase of free colored persons in those States. In 1850, one seventh of their total colored population was free.

This peaceable progress of Freedom may also be seen in the number of manumissions. The Border States suffer the most from the loss of fugitive slaves; still, in them the number of manumissions is far larger than the number of fugitives.

The Border States seem thus to be very intimately connected with their Northern neighbors. Their commerce, their population, their history, their geographical position, and their whole progress point to the North and to Union. Ambitious politicians may, perhaps, for a while misguide the people of some of those States, but they can not blind them, for any considerable time, to their real interests. They know, too, that should they remain in the Union, the greatest delicacy would be shown to them. As Slave States they would then be in a small minority; but this very fact would obliterate Slavery as a basis of party distinction. There would be one common country, and all its parts would faithfully do their duty toward one another, in strict conformance to the dictates of the Constitution.

There are then the States of TENNESSEE and ARKANSAS. They show in everything their close connection with Kentucky and Missouri, and with the great Valley of the Mississippi, whose fate they must share. The free West and two flourishing Border States on their North, Louisiana, with its increasing white population, on their South, and the unbroken Mississippi, will, we hope, be fetters strong enough to keep those two States also from violently leaving the Union.

And now there are six States left, the two CAROLINAS and the EASTERN GULF STATES! Why should *they* wish to secede? Are there not in their history additional reasons which should make them both wise and grateful?

Has it not been demonstrated over and over again that the South, both in peace and in war, has ever derived the greatest material advantages from being in the Union? What is the injury which they have now received at the hands of the North? The election of a Republican President? No; this accidental occasion, selected for secession, can not be called even the near cause. It is of importance only insomuch as it fixes the date of the event. The President-elect has repeatedly declared himself in favor of a strict adherence to a constitutional Fugitive Slave Law. He has gone still further, and frankly expressed his opinion to be that the United States, as such, has nothing to do with Slavery where it exists. He, then, stands on a platform which contains not the faintest whisper of Abolition sentiments. He is the standard-bearer of a party which—in order to show the South that they were no Abolitionists—committed the indelicacy of dragging JOHN BROWN, who had duly been caught, tried, sentenced, hung, and buried, from an "honorable" solitude into a public platform. The only crime of the President-elect is that he does not subscribe to a policy which would perpetuate civil war on the outskirts of our empire, and drench every new inch of ground, gained for civilization, with the blood of murdered citizens. And as for his party, it has not the ascendancy in Congress, nor in the Supreme Court of the United States. What hurt could it do, even if it wished to do hurt? Or has it not as much right to extend Freedom as other parties have to extend Slavery? But is it not ready to submit to all the demands of the Constitution? Or if this displeasure with the Republican party is a mere pretext, is the South angry because she can no longer keep up the abnormal balance between Slavery and Freedom? What power can check the natural and constitutional growth of the latter? Are the Border States worse off on account of the increase of their free population? No; this whole question of Freedom and Slavery has its warlike features only through political interference. Let the policy of the United States in respect to it be once firmly settled, then an enlightened and dispassionate South will no more growl because of the fruits of Freedom. It will understand that the very power of the United States which it now tries to overthrow, is the guardian of its peaceable development.

V.—PROGNOSTIC OF A SOUTHERN HEXARCHY.

To secede and to recede are the self-same thing. Slavery can no longer continue the struggle against Freedom. It leaves the battle-field, and its arms are henceforth turned no more against the North, but against its own self. For secession is a suicidal policy. Where is the wealth, where the labor, to build up a separate Confederacy? Where are their bread and their clothes? Who will work in their manufactories? Who will be their sailors? White laborers will shun their land. The free colored people will flee from fear of being enslaved. And what an industrial independence that would be! They have cotton and some minor products to exchange; but woe to a nation that raises but one principal product! It will be Free in nothing, and Slave in everything. Still, these things might gradually be changed; but where and who are the men who will make this change under a separate empire?

We will add a few tables.

TABLE XXVIII.—POPULATION OF THE TWO CAROLINAS AND OF THE EASTERN GULF STATES IN 1850.

States.	Whites.	Free Colored.	Slaves.	Total Colored.	Total.
N. Carolina..	553,000	27,400	288,500	315,900	869,000
S. Carolina...	274,500	8,900	384,900	393,800	668,500
Georgia......	521,500	2,900	381,600	384,500	906,100
Florida......	47,200	900	39,300	40,200	87,400
Alabama....	426,500	2,200	342,800	345,000	771,600
Mississippi...	295,700	900	309,800	410,700	606,300
Total.....	2,118,600	43,200	1,746,900	1,790,100	3,908,000

TABLE XXIX.—PROPORTION OF WHITE TO TOTAL POPULATION. (IN PER CENTS.)

States.	1790.	1800.	1810.	1820.	1830.	1840.	1850.
North Carolina....	73.19	70.65	67.76	65.62	64.07	64.36	63.64
South Carolina....	56.28	56.79	51.60	47.33	44.37	43.59	41.07
Georgia...........	64.07	62.73	57.60	55.59	57.43	58.97	57.56
Florida...........	—	—	—	—	52.93	51.29	53.98
Alabama	—	—	—	66.81	61.52	56.74	55.27
Mississippi........	—	58.52	57.06	55.90	51.56	47.67	48.76

TABLE XXX.—PROPORTION OF FREE COLORED TO TOTAL POPULATION.

States.	1790.	1800.	1810.	1820.	1830.	1840.	1850.
North Carolina ..	1.26	1.47	1.85	2.29	2.65	3.01	3.16
South Carolina...	0.72	0.92	1.10	1.36	1.36	1.39	1.34
Georgia..........	0.48	0.63	0.71	0.51	0 48	0.40	0.32
Florida...........	—	—	—	—	2.43	1.50	1.07
Alabama	—	—	—	0.45	0.51	0.34	0.29
Mississippi	—	2.06	0.59	0.61	0 38	0.36	0.15

TABLE XXXI.—MANUMITTED AND FUGITVE SLAVES IN 1850.

States.	Slaves.	Manumitted.	Fugitives.
North Carolina.	288,500	2	64
South Carolina...	384,400	2	16
Georgia	381,600	19	89
Florida...............	39,300	22	18
Alabama	342,800	29	16
Mississippi............	309,800	6	41
	1,746,900	67	257

These tables show that the six States together had, in 1850, a population about equal in number to that of the United States when they were first founded. The ingenious Superintendent of the Census of 1850 makes the whole Gulf States a rather dubious compliment when he says, "that while the Atlantic States have increased more than threefold since 1790, the Gulf States, which had then scarcely any existence, have now a population of nearly one half as great as the population of all the States together at that time." But that "*whole* population of all the States at that time" was indeed very small, and one half of that is scarcely large enough to build up a separate nation.

The rate of increase, too, is not so very favorable. The Gulf, east of the Mississippi, increased, on the whole, only 6.1 per cent., while the Atlantic Slope increased 54.8 per cent., and the Mississippi Valley 37.2 per cent. If we add to the Gulf States, east of the Mississippi, the two Carolinas, the proportions will change but little. For the ratio of the decennial increase steadily and rapidly diminished in North Carolina from 21.42 per cent. in 1800 to 15.35 in 1850; and in South Carolina, from 38.75 per cent. in 1800 to 12.47 in 1850. Now, should those six States even grow at the same ratio as they have done heretofore, and the colored people be counted as regular population, it would take them at least six times as long as it did the Valley of the Mississippi and the Atlantic Slope to grow to *their* number and strength. They would thus reach, in about 300 or 400 years, the present power of the United States, of which they are now already a part, and whose influence, and glory, and position in the world they now share as coëqual members. To say the least, secession on their part is exceedingly impolitic. They would at once sink from being a great power in the world to a fourth-rate little State, with no voice or influence in the life of nations.

But there is another aspect to these tables. It appears that the proportion of the white population in these States is continually growing smaller, a phenomenon very different from what was seen in the Border States.

From the first year of computation to 1850 that proportion decreased in

N. Carolina.	S. Carolina.	Georgia.	Florida.	Alabama.	Mississippi.
9.55 per cent.	15.21	6.51	(incr.) 1.05	11.54.	9.76

The mean decrease of the proportion of white to total population in the six States together is thus 8.43 per cent. The proportion of free colored persons to total population is also steadily decreasing, except in North Carolina; nor are there any manumissions worth mentioning. The slaves will thus be in a majority long before the Confederacy reaches any considerable power in the world. And what will be the result of such an increase?

The news of a separation from the original republic of the United States can not even now be kept a secret from the slave population. It has reached them through the patriotic speeches of indignant Southerners, through the misrepresentations of an enraged party press, through the whispers of their free colored brethren. Though they are at present but partially informed, they would soon better appreciate their position. The United States would be to them a second England. No fugitive slave law would help the slaveholder of a Southern republic to obtain his runaway Negroes from the then foreign soil of the United States. Nor would the loss of Negroes be their only disadvantage. The slaves would soon awaken to a consciousness of their power, and break out in open rebellion. No United States would then be the guardian of the slave power. No United States posse would be found to subdue the insurrection.

And should this be false prophecy, and the Negroes

remain peaceable, and increase in number, what will the South do with that increased number? There would be no more new territory for the slave power to conquer and colonize. The United States, England, and France would then go hand in hand, and no WALKER would ever again dare to think of putting Slavery where formerly Freedom was. The world has hitherto appreciated the difficult position of the United States, and its committal to Slavery. The world has been forced to respect the United States as a Great Power, and has feared its strength. The world endured much from it, in order to avoid collisions detrimental to all. But things would look differently in case of a permanent secession. The Great Powers of the world, and especially England and the United States, would then be united, and jointly watch over the fortunes of races and nations.

But a Southern Confederacy would not so long exist, even should it be joined by several more or by all the Slave States. FR. LIST's words would soon be applicable to them: "The debt which so greatly oppresses them is the result of a series of excessive exertions to maintain their independence, and it is in the nature of things that the evil should reach a point where it may be intolerable, and when their incorporation into a greater nationality would appear as acceptable as it will be necessary." Troubles from within and troubles from without would soon prove to them the fatality of secession. The poetical excitement of the first days would soon pass away, and prosy misery take its place. Long before a dreaded slave insurrection would strike horror into the breast of the South and of the whole world—long before the Southern republic would wage war against a world in arms—parties would arise within their own precincts, and the cry of Union, no more fearing to be choked as treason, would be again heard from the Gulf of Mexico to the borders of Old Virginia, from the Mississippi to the mighty oceans; and the glorious Republic of the United States of America would be one again and forever.

VI.—A NEW PROPOSAL FOR A COMPROMISE.

Experiments of Disunion with their different contingencies are costly and unfortunate. They bring distress on all sections. It would take years to recover from such a violent disrupture of a country—of its industry, of its commerce, and of its government. But still, in the end, the South would lose the most; for there is, even in the worst case of secession—a secession of all the Slave States—more wealth and more productive labor, more strength and more power to rely upon in the North than in the South.

TABLE XXXII.—PROGRESS OF POPULATION.

SLAVE STATES.	FREE STATES.
1790............1,271,500	1790............1,901,000
1800............1,703,000	1800............2,601,500
1810............2,208,800	1810............3,653,200
1820............2,831,600	1820............5,030,400
1830............3,662,600	1830............6,874,800
1840............4,634,500	1840............9,561,200
1850............6,222,400	1850............13,330,600

The difference between the numbers of whites in the Slave and in the Free States was thus about 700,000 in 1790. The difference in 1850 was about 7,000,000, and it must be still greater in 1860; for the rate of increase of the Slave States was in the last decade 34.26 per cent.; of the Free States 39.42. Thus the whites in the South will number, in 1860, about 8,338,000, and those in the

North about 18,529,500. Moreover, in case of Disunion, that gradual and peaceable pressing down into the Southern States would cease; the North would keep its full numbers and spread on its own soil, and thus increase at a still higher ratio, while all emancipation would at once stop, and be replaced by violent insurrection.

We confined ourselves in our last reasonings, about population to white men; for in case of Disunion there would but little reliance be placed on the colored persons, be it in peace or in war.

But we think so highly of the Union, we are so well aware of the advantages accruing from it to the whole country and to the world, we feel so keenly the evils from Disunion (though it be but partial and momentary), that, should our old Constitution not suffice, we would be willing, at any time, to submit to a new compromise. Nay, further, we would be ready, for the sake of union and peace, to yield our whole point respecting Slavery, and to look henceforth at the slave, politically, or rather internationally, as a mere beast or other property, such as an ass or horse is. But, in subscribing thus to the opinions of the South, we would ask in return for a *rigid adherence to this Southern principle in all its logical consequences.* We would therefore propose the following amendment to the Constitution, short, simple, and radical:

Whereas, The present provisions in the Constitution, as far as they refer to slaves, viz., " persons bound to service," have, during an experience of seventy years, proved to be inadequate for preventing dissension and violence consequent on the question of Slavery in these United States;

Whereas, Those provisions even now prove insufficient

longer to satisfy the North and the South in such manner as that they may remain united;

Resolved, That, in Art. I., Sec. 2, ¶ 3, beginning thus: "Representatives and direct taxes shall be apportioned among the several States which may be included within this Union, according to their respective numbers," the following words be stricken out, namely: "which shall be determined by adding to the whole number of free persons, including those bound to service for a term of years, and excluding Indians not taxed, three fifths of all other persons."

Resolved, That, Art. IV., Sec. 2, ¶ 3, reading thus: "No person held to service or labor in one State, under the laws thereof, escaping into another, shall, in consequence of any law or regulation therein, be discharged from such service or labor, but shall be delivered up on claim of the party to whom such service or labor may be due," be likewise stricken out.

Resolved, That in lieu of the last-named paragraph (namely, Art. IV., Sec. 2, ¶ 3), the following be substituted:

"¶ 3. Whatever is regarded as property under the laws of one State, shall also be regarded as such in all the other States."

This would be in perfect accordance with Mr. DAVIS' resolutions in the Senate Committee of Thirteen.

"Mr. DAVIS offered the following resolution, which lies over with the others:

"That it shall be declared by amendment of the Constitution that property in slaves, recognized as such by the local law of any of the States of the Union, shall stand upon the same footing in all constitutional and federal relations as any other species of property so recognized; and, like other property, shall not be subject to be divested or impaired by the local law of any other State either in escape thereto, or by the transit or sojourn of the owner therein. And in no case whatever shall such property be subject to be divested or impaired by any legislative act of the United States, or any of the territories thereof."

The Fugitive Slave Law, which is based on Art. IV., Sec. 2, ¶ 3, would then be invalid. The North would no more be called upon to fulfill the unpleasant duty of catching fugitive slaves. The owner alone would be responsible for all possible losses of horses, asses, or slaves.

The Southerner, on the other side, might henceforth, undisturbed by any Personal Liberty Bill or "erroneous" interpretation of the Constitution, go with his property—ass, horse, or slave—wherever he chose—to any State or Territory, settled or unsettled. But he himself must henceforth take care of his property. If it be stolen or injured, he can apply to the proper authorities; but if it runs away, from its own free wish and will, he himself must run after it, and catch it, and drive it home again. His neighbors may lend him kind assistance if they choose, but they will not legally or constitutionally be bound to do it.

The number of Southern representatives to Congress would also be somewhat diminished by carrying out the Southern doctrine in all its logical consequences. This would be unpleasant; but there would be no help for it. Other deductions might be made from the same principle; but as they would chiefly refer to the internal affairs of each State, they are omitted in this general compromise.

Nor would it be to the disadvantage of the Negro slave; for the chances of freedom would be, by far, greater for him in the Free States than in the Slave States. This political nationalization of Slavery would even hasten the work of emancipation; for the influence of the free white *population would thereby become more direct.* Suppose the State of New York should in such a way receive some 10,000 slaves. They would certainly be prepared for freedom and become free in a shorter time here than if they had remained in South Carolina.

Nor would this dispersion of slaves over the whole national territory add anything to our disgrace, if such it be to own slaves. We have the same responsibility, and deserve the same epithets, whether our Slavery is in sixteen States only or in thirty-four: for we are one common *nation*. The question is only, how we can best secure its gradual abolition.

CONCLUSION.

So much for compromises. But until it is decided whether the original Constitution or the amended one shall henceforth be the Supreme Law of the land, the proper policy of the United States Government is as clear and distinct as its right and duty.

Whatever the future may bring, peace or war, the United States must—

1. Keep, defend, and in case of treason or defeat, retake, at any cost, all *national* fortifications necessary for the protection of all her old boundaries, and for common national safety.

2. She must keep, defend, and, in case of necessity, retake, at any cost, the Mississippi from its source to its mouth.

3. She must, in all other respects, leave the States undisturbed in their *internal* process of secession, unless they attack national property.

4. She must give the secessionary States time to recover from their excitement, and leave to them the same *initiatory*

step in returning to the Union that they assumed in seceding from it.

This must be the present course of action on the part of the United States. It follows from the constitutional principle of *Protection to National Interest and Non-Interference with Local Matters*, and will probably cover all future contingencies.

Should, however, the present force of the United States army, from any reason, be inadequate to the above task, there would be enough patriotism left in the land to call, at the shortest notice, a million of men to arms, who, without distinction of party, would be ready to fight for this common country, and rout the rebels, from whatever section they might come.

THE END.

Printed in Dunstable, United Kingdom